THE SUPERNATURAL POWER OF

# JESUS'
# BLOOD

THE SUPERNATURAL POWER OF

# JESUS' BLOOD

*Applying the Blessings Available Through Jesus' Blood*

# HANK KUNNEMAN

DESTINY IMAGE® PUBLISHERS, INC.

P.O. Box 310, Shippensburg, PA 17257-0310

*"Promoting Inspired Lives."*

This book and all other Destiny Image and Destiny Image Fiction books are available at Christian bookstores and distributors worldwide.

For more information on foreign distributors, call 717-532-3040.

Reach us on the Internet: www.destinyimage.com.

ISBN 13 TP: 978-0-7684-6147-3
ISBN 13 eBook: 978-0-7684-6242-5
ISBN 13 HC: 978-0-7684-6244-9
ISBN 13 LP: 978-0-7684-6243-2

For Worldwide Distribution, Printed in the U.S.A.

1 2 3 4 5 6 7 8 / 26 25 24 23 22

# CONTENTS

Foreword . . . . . . . . . . . . . . . . . . . . . . . . . 1

**PART 1**  Understanding Your Blood Covenant Rights
and Privileges . . . . . . . . . . . . . . . . . . . . . . . . . 3

CHAPTER ONE       The Life-Giving Blood . . . . . . . . . . . . . . . . 5

CHAPTER TWO       The Covenant Blood. . . . . . . . . . . . . . . . 23

CHAPTER THREE     The Overcoming Blood . . . . . . . . . . . . . . 51

CHAPTER FOUR      The Shed Blood . . . . . . . . . . . . . . . . . . 67

CHAPTER FIVE      The Sprinkled Blood. . . . . . . . . . . . . . . . 83

**PART 2**  Blood, Water, Spirit: Our Pattern for
Abundant Life . . . . . . . . . . . . . . . . . . . . . . . . . 99

CHAPTER SIX       These Three Agree: The Blood, Water,
and Spirit . . . . . . . . . . . . . . . . . . . . . . . . . 101

CHAPTER SEVEN     The Prophetic Pattern of the Blood, Water,
and Spirit . . . . . . . . . . . . . . . . . . . . . . . . . 115

CHAPTER EIGHT     Pentecost and the Blood, Water,
and Spirit . . . . . . . . . . . . . . . . . . . . . . . . . 133

CHAPTER NINE      Pentecost and the Approval of God . . . . 145

CHAPTER TEN       The Holy Spirit Baptism and Adding
Our Agreement . . . . . . . . . . . . . . . . . . . . 161

# FOREWORD

*"And they overcame him by the blood of the Lamb."* Those words should be enough to provoke a great passion in you to understand the Blood of Jesus.

Only God knows how many needless agonies and defeats we have endured because we did not understand or honor the surpassing power of Christ's Blood.

In every century when the church honored the power of the Blood, she advanced and took territories for the Kingdom of God. In the centuries when the precious Blood has been ignored or dishonored, the church has been neutralized or driven underground.

We have lost key battles and valuable ground in our culture. We have seen a surge of believers wounded and weak. How can we deny the connection? The more we have neglected the power of the Blood, the more we have lost on the battlefield.

No wonder the devil has taken great pains to bury this sacred truth. No wonder he strives to make us ashamed! Isn't it time you grasped why the Blood of Christ terrifies satan?

The revelation of the Blood of Christ is such a key that I can confidently say you do not want either victory or breakthrough unless you seek to understand the power of the Blood.

Hank Kunneman is handing you a priceless gift. He has done it in clear and concise language. Few books are as needed today as this one. Sit down and read this book. It will not just change your life, it will make you armed and dangerous.

MARIO MURILLO

PART 1

# UNDERSTANDING YOUR BLOOD COVENANT RIGHTS AND PRIVILEGES

3

# CHAPTER ONE

# THE LIFE-GIVING BLOOD

As a young boy, even before I had given my life to the Lord, I would hear one of my relatives talk about the Blood of Jesus and was even taught the importance of pleading the Blood. Even though I didn't know the Lord and what I was really doing, I would plead the Blood of Jesus over my car when I would go places. I must admit I was fascinated by this subject, and even more so why someone named Jesus Christ would come to this earth and shed His life-giving Blood for me. Since I was saved, I have found the Blood of Jesus to be one of my favorite topics to discuss and preach. There is so much we have been freely given because of His precious Blood that was shed for us.

This is because God has provided our complete freedom and victory through Jesus' Blood. It is the most sacred, important message in Scripture. His Blood is life-giving Blood! Unfortunately, in our culture the Blood of Jesus is often disregarded, cheapened, and misunderstood. Some churches are even taking songs about the Blood out of their hymnals, calling it "grotesque." But our faith is established on this very Blood. Without Jesus' Blood, we have nothing! It's made us clean and righteous; it's given us the ability to live above the curse of sin. The Blood of Jesus has put us in an eternal position of power and authority as God has *raised us up together, and made us sit together in heavenly places in Christ Jesus*" (Eph. 2:6). Do you see that? In these heavenly places, we are *above* the natural realm; we are above all the works of the enemy, and we have ultimate authority over him! (See Luke 10:19.)

We need to think rightly about Jesus' Blood. It is critical in the days in which we live that born-again believers walk in a greater understanding of the power of this precious, life-giving Blood. Many Christians don't often stop to consider its power or know how to activate it in their daily lives. We don't just need to know *about* it; we need to activate its supernatural work in our lives every day! It's available *to* us and *for* us, but we must choose to live in the blessings of our Blood covenant.

Jesus tells us in John 10:10 that the devil comes "*to steal, and to kill, and to destroy: I am come that they might have life, and that they might have it more abundantly!*" It is our job to defend the blessings Jesus has provided through the power of His shed Blood. It's up to us to choose to walk in the abundant life He died to give us. There is supernatural power that is activated in our lives as we align ourselves (our thoughts, words, and actions) with the truth that is found in our Blood covenant.

I want you to walk in greater victory than you've ever known and to experience the tremendous benefits the Blood provides to every born-again child of God! As we look at the Blood covenant the Lord has made with us through His Son, I pray that you see life and death, blessings and curses are before you every day, and that you always choose life! (See Deuteronomy 30.) It is life that comes from His life-giving Blood that was shed for us.

The story of the Blood began before the foundation of the earth was formed.

> *And all that dwell upon the earth shall worship him* [beast], *whose names are not written in the book of life of the Lamb slain from the foundation of the world* (Revelation 13:8).

How sobering it is when we realize that God the Father had already planned to sacrifice His only Son for us before He formed the world! The Blood was decided on and offered by God before He set the universe in motion. Jesus' Blood would not be a chance encounter with humanity. God stood at the beginning of time and looked down through all of history and, knowing what was coming, He carefully planned the rescue He knew we'd need!

Through the life-giving Blood of Jesus, He made provision for every detail of the redemption of every generation throughout history. Have you ever thought about how costly it was for God to make man? It was costly because man would have free will, and with that free will he would sin, opening the door to eternal separation from God. This was never God's intention. His heart's greatest intention was to be joined with us forever, and because of His tremendous love He was prepared to pay the price for His children—His very own Blood.

> *Behold what manner of love the Father has bestowed on us, that we should be called children of God!* (1 John 3:1a NKJV).

## THE LIFE IS IN THE BLOOD

Before man ever had breath in his body, God had determined that the life of the flesh would be in the blood (see Lev. 17). We know this because the Lamb was slain *before* the foundation of the world (see Rev. 13:8).

It was the breath of God that brought Adam to life when God breathed into his nostrils. We often think that what God did with Adam looked like mouth-to-mouth resuscitation or CPR, but I believe God was already living inside of Adam and God breathed *out* of Adam's nostrils, giving him his very first breath and causing blood to flow into every vein of his body (see Gen. 2:7). The Hebrew word for *breathed* in this verse is *naphach* and means *"to cause to breathe out"* (Strong's #H5301). Blood carries breath (oxygen) throughout the body and sustains life.

When God breathed, blood began to flow in Adam and he became alive. Adam was brought into spiritual life *and* natural life when God breathed that day. Imagine how the Lord felt when He saw the man's eyes open, his chest begin to breathe with His life, and his heart begin to beat signifying life! Blood was flowing through this man, Adam, and life was given to him by God's very breath. This same man now alive would have the very God of all creation die for him and all mankind now that blood had flowed, giving life to man.

The name *Adam* in Hebrew means "red man or blood man" (Strong's #H121). He was the very first man whose blood carried life throughout his body, as God had already ordained that the *life* would be in the *blood*.

> *For the life of the flesh is in the blood: and I have given it to you upon the altar to make an atonement for your souls: for it is the blood that maketh an atonement for the soul* (Leviticus 17:11).

The Hebrew word for *atonement* here is *kaphar*, and it means "to cover over, to atone for sin and persons by legal rites" (Strong's #H3722). Atonement was good; it meant their sins were covered, but that's where it stopped. When Jesus was offered as the sacrifice for our sins, His Blood did more than atone for our sins—it completely removed them!

> *As far as the east is from the west, so far hath he removed our transgressions from us* (Psalm 103:12).

This means that God is not keeping a list to hold against you! This is why He has cast our sins not north and south, where it can be measured and found, but east and west, which speaks of no reference point to be measured or found. If you are living in regret over things from your past, it's time to let those things go. The "past" is any time prior to the moment you're in right now! Don't hold on to your own sin—let it go. When you remind God of your sin, you are bringing accusation against yourself and coming into agreement with the enemy, who is *"the accuser of our brethren"* (Rev. 12:10). Don't live under accusation—go to Scripture to see who God says you are as His covenant heir and determine to agree with Him!

Our need for a Savior, the Messiah Jesus, to shed His innocent, precious Blood and redeem us began when Adam and Eve sinned in the Garden. Through that one act, they opened the door to death for themselves and every generation that would follow. When they sinned, their *true* life was no longer in their blood. Instead, their blood became polluted and deserving of death. From that first sin, our sin nature was introduced and now *"all have sinned"* (Rom. 3:23). *"Through the trespass of one man came condemnation for all men"* (Rom. 5:18b MEV).

This sin nature would mean that every person born into the earth from that point on would be born with polluted blood. This brought a curse of sickness, mental oppression, anxiety, fears, and all the things the enemy uses to harass us. But God saw our condition and came to our rescue!

*When I passed by you and saw you polluted in your own blood, I said to you when you were in your blood, "Live!" Indeed, I said to you when you were in your blood, "Live!"* (Ezekiel 16:6 MEV).

Because God had originally put life in the blood, pure and unpolluted blood was the only way to restore true life. A blood sacrifice would be required to redeem mankind from the curse of sin.

*Without the shedding of blood there is no forgiveness* (Hebrews 9:22b MEV).

The curse came through a man, so the breaking of the curse would require a sinless Man to come and shed His Blood. As we mentioned, it would be the Lamb of God, slain even before the foundations of the world, who would be the one chosen to redeem all mankind. This is why, since the Garden of Eden, we know that there has only ever been One Man born with unpolluted Blood to pay the penalty of man's sin—Jesus Christ. *"Through the righteous act of One came justification of life for all men"* (Rom. 5:18 MEV). This is why the Father's cry to us to *"Live!"* echoes throughout eternity through Jesus' sacrifice on the cross.

*Neither by the blood of goats and calves, but by His own blood, He entered the Most Holy Place once for all, having obtained eternal redemption* (Hebrews 9:12 MEV).

Remember, God had *already* made provision to give us life *"from the foundation of the world"* (Rev. 13:8). Out of His great heart of love, God *already* had a plan set in place to rescue us, and it had to do with shedding His own innocent Blood.

> *For as by one man's disobedience many were made sinners, so by the obedience of one shall many be made righteous* (Romans 5:19).

God's plan was that we'd be justified and brought back from death to life by Jesus' sacrifice. The price sin demands is death, but God has always been willing to pay the price for us to have abundant life—through the covenant of His Son's unpolluted shed Blood!

## THREE GARDENS

God clearly and powerfully demonstrates His plan to cleanse and restore us back into right relationship with Him in three gardens throughout Scripture: Eden, Gethsemane, and at the Garden Tomb, where Jesus first appeared to Mary after His resurrection. These three gardens paint a prophetic picture of Jesus restoring what Adam lost.

First, the Garden of Eden was originally our Paradise; it was literally heaven on earth—a place Adam and Eve were to steward, and where they enjoyed perfect fellowship with God the Father. But when Adam and Eve sinned, it broke that perfect fellowship and God actually showed mercy by removing them from the Garden. If God had allowed them to stay, they likely would have eaten from the tree of life, causing them to *physically* live forever in their fallen state. In His mercy, God prevented that from happening by sending them out of Eden.

> *And the Lord God said, Behold, the man is become as one of us, to know good and evil: and now, lest he put forth his hand, and take also of the tree of life, and eat, and live for ever: therefore the Lord God sent him forth from the garden of Eden, to till the ground from whence he was taken* (Genesis 3:22-23).

Eden represents the blessed life that comes when we are in right standing with God. When Adam and Eve lost that fellowship and were removed from the Garden, all humanity lost that right standing as well. It is only by the Blood of Jesus that we can be restored to our "Eden" and brought back into perfect fellowship with the Father. The next two gardens, Gethsemane and the Garden Tomb, are New Testament pictures of this restoration.

In the New Testament, the Garden of Gethsemane was a place of intense pain, darkness, and agony for Jesus. It represents the suffering of mankind that came with our broken fellowship with God—a result of the first sin. Remember that Jesus sweat drops of Blood in Gethsemane. Gethsemane points us to the Blood that would wash away the suffering, stress, and pain we all experience. At the same time, Jesus' Blood made Gethsemane the entryway for us back into Paradise, or our "Eden" of right relationship with the Father. Through Jesus' shed Blood, Gethsemane reminds us that our suffering and broken fellowship with God were fully put upon Him.

The third garden was the Garden Tomb, where Jesus' body was laid after He was crucified. The Garden Tomb is a picture of our fully restored "Eden." It represents our being brought back into right fellowship with God. We can see this a little more clearly if we look back at the Garden of Eden.

In Genesis 2:15, God had given man the responsibility of tending the Garden of Eden: "*And the Lord God took the man, and put him into the garden of Eden to dress it and to keep it.*" Two words describe Adam's original responsibilities in the Garden:

1. *Dress* is the Hebrew word *abad,* meaning "to labor, to serve (God); to serve (with Levitical service); to make oneself a servant" (Strong's #H5647).

2. *Keep* is the Hebrew word *shamar* and it means "to keep, have charge of; to keep, guard, keep watch and ward, protect, save life" (Strong's #H8104).

Adam was given the task of being the gardener in Eden. He was to keep the garden, protect it, and watch over it, but he failed to do these things. The Bible calls Jesus the "second Adam" or "last Adam" (see Rom. 5:12-21). Jesus was the second "gardener" who would not fail to keep and protect the garden or fall out of fellowship with the Father.

Notice that when He appears to Mary at the Garden Tomb, she thinks He is the gardener!

> *Jesus said to her, "Woman, why are you weeping? Whom are you seeking?" Supposing Him to be the gardener, she said to Him, "Sir, if You have carried Him away, tell me where You have put Him, and I will take Him away"* (John 20:15 MEV).

In fact, Jesus *was* the Gardener—the One who made Himself a servant (*abad*). He was the One who was keeping watch and providing protection (*shamar*)! He kept the garden secure and His fellowship with God was never broken. Further on in the story, Jesus offers that same perfect fellowship with God to Mary.

> *Jesus said to her, "Do not cling to Me, for I have not yet ascended to My Father; but go to My brethren and say to them, 'I am ascending to My Father and your Father, and to My God and your God'"* (John 20:17 NKJV).

Jesus is offering Mary a place of restored fellowship, but pay close attention to His words. He mentions God *first* as her Father, and *then* refers to His deity (God). He is telling her that fellowship with God the Father is being brought back to the personal level that Adam first enjoyed before he sinned. Our covenant is first with Him as our Father, and then with Him as our God. The revelation of His fatherhood helps us to better understand His deity. This place of perfect fellowship is the "Eden" that Jesus restored!

Finally, Gethsemane and the Garden Tomb relate to Eden because the curse of man's labor and toil was redeemed by what Jesus did in these two places. The Garden of Gethsemane shows us the pain and toil that required His Blood for redemption, and that redemption was finalized by the time Jesus appeared to Mary at the Garden Tomb. In Eden, God told Adam:

> *Cursed is the ground on account of you; in hard labor you will eat of it all the days of your life. Thorns and thistles it will bring forth for you, and you will eat the plants of the field. By the sweat of your face you will eat bread until you return to the ground* (Genesis 3:17b-19a MEV).

The Lord told Adam that the results of sin would include the ground being cursed and man having to labor and sweat to cause the land to produce. But look at Jesus' redemptive act as He prayed in Gethsemane:

> *And being in anguish, He prayed more earnestly. And His sweat became like great drops of blood falling down to the ground* (Luke 22:44 MEV).

Jesus labored in anguish as He prayed; the sweat of His face became His own Blood falling to the ground. When this happened, it was representative of the sweat of man's brow, or his hard toil of life, being broken (see Gen. 3:18-19).

The progression from original sin to perfect redemption is shown in these three gardens. In Eden, our fellowship with God was broken, causing us to live under the toil and burden of sin. But Gethsemane and the Garden Tomb show us how Jesus' shed Blood beautifully restored us to perfect relationship with the Father!

## OUR RIGHTEOUSNESS

We were never intended to atone for our own sin. In fact, we've never been able to do that. God didn't design it that way; He knew we'd need a Savior. He tells us that our righteous acts are as filthy rags (see Isa. 64:6). Our righteous acts are not clothing that we can wear, and they can never reverse our condition of polluted blood. But since the beginning, we've certainly worked hard trying to produce our own righteousness!

Sometimes we feel like we have to pray enough, fast enough, give enough in order to get God to respond to us. We don't always realize we may be trying to produce our own righteousness by doing these things. I'm not saying we shouldn't pray, or fast, or give. Absolutely we should do these things—Jesus told us to! But our motivation needs to come from love *for* Him rather than trying to get something *from* Him! Whenever we're doing things to earn something from God, God calls those dead works. But by His Blood, Jesus has cleansed our conscience from dead works so that we can serve the living God (see Heb. 9:14).

> *And the eyes of them both were opened, and they knew that they were naked; and they sewed fig leaves together, and made themselves aprons* (Genesis 3:7).

Adam and Eve sewing fig leaves together is a picture of us as humans trying to cover our own sin. Just as they sought the covering and protection of the fig leaves, our righteous acts can never provide what we really need. We cannot produce righteousness on our own. We cannot cover ourselves with anything more than fig leaves (filthy rags).

But look what God does! He quickly steps in and makes clothing for them in Genesis 3:21: *"Unto Adam also and to his wife did the Lord God make coats of skins, and clothed them."*

*How* God makes this covering is significant. Notice it was made of animal skin. This was the very first blood sacrifice. These animal skins would have been dripping in blood, a demonstration of the Blood covenant that was required for our redemption. It's a powerful picture of the Lamb who would be slain to cover all our sin and give us life again!

For Adam and Eve, this first sacrifice covered their nakedness (shame/sin). But God also provided the *last* and forever-complete sacrifice—Jesus! Under Jesus' Blood, God's covenant provides even more than our covering—He changes us into new creations, forgiving our shame and sin! We are covered *and* made righteous through His Blood. We aren't *under* the righteousness of God; we *are* the righteousness of God!

> *For he hath made him to be sin for us, who knew no sin; that we might be made the righteousness of God in him* (2 Corinthians 5:21).

## NATHANAEL UNDER THE FIG TREE

In the Garden of Eden, fig leaves represented man's feeble efforts to cover himself. In the New Testament, Jesus makes two key references to a fig tree, giving us a more complete picture of ourselves and our attempts at self-righteousness.

First, when Jesus sees Nathanael, He tells him that He had seen him *"under the fig tree"* (John 1:48). When Adam and Eve tried to hide under fig leaves, every future generation was hiding there with them because all of humanity had fallen under the curse of sin that day.

> *Nathanael saith unto him, Whence knowest thou me? Jesus answered and said unto him, Before that Philip called thee, when thou wast under the fig tree, I saw thee* (John 1:48).

The Greek word for *saw* is *eido,* and it means "to perceive by any of the senses; to ascertain what must be done about it; to have regard for one, cherish, pay attention to" (Strong's #G1492). Jesus saw us all under the fig leaves in the Garden of Eden; He knew what must be done to remedy our condition, and He loved us enough to pour out His own Blood to rescue us from sin and death! Nathanael under the fig tree is a picture of us trying to hide or cover our own sin and our need to come to Jesus as he did. Regardless of where we are, Jesus sees. He knows where we are, and this is good news! *"While we were yet sinners, Christ died for us"* (Rom. 5:8).

Jesus has never been afraid of our sin. When we were still in our sin hiding under our own fig leaves like Adam and Eve or the fig tree like Nathaniel, He loved us unconditionally! Do you ever find yourself "hiding" from the Lord? It is a beautiful thing that He sees even the things we don't want Him to see. He is our Father and He is Love and Light. Whatever you may be walking through, He sees. He sees your problem, and He sees your heart. When you may not know what to do, He *eidos* you—He knows what to do about your situation, and He loves you so much that He will always provide a rescue!

## Jesus Curses the Fig Tree

The second time Jesus mentions a fig tree, He curses it because it is bearing no fruit.

> *And when he saw a fig tree in the way, he came to it, and found nothing thereon, but leaves only, and said unto it, Let no fruit grow on thee henceforward for ever. And presently the fig tree withered away* (Matthew 21:19).

This fig tree represents man's own righteousness that can never produce living fruit. The picture in the Garden of Eden is Adam and Eve wearing *"leaves only,"* a symbol of their lives not bearing any fruit. The prophetic application of Nathaniel under a fig tree speaks of our life that is unfruitful or the fruit we think we are bearing in this life. We still must come and surrender to Jesus as He is the

Way, the Truth, and the Life. A life apart from Him is a cursed life like the fig tree producing little to no fruit without the Lord.

Scripture says that "*presently*" (immediately) the fig tree withered away when Jesus cursed it. He uses this demonstration to teach His disciples a lesson on faith.

> *Jesus answered and said unto them, Verily I say unto you, If ye have faith, and doubt not, ye shall not only do this which is done to the fig tree, but also if ye shall say unto this mountain, Be thou removed, and be thou cast into the sea; it shall be done* (Matthew 21:21).

*Immediately* when we put our faith in Jesus, we are no longer under our own feeble efforts of self-righteousness. This tree of our dead works that bears no fruit *immediately* withers away. Jesus also speaks of our new authority in Him—when we are born again, we are new creations, the righteousness of God. *Now* when we speak to mountains from our position of faith as new creations under the Blood covenant, they will move!

> *Therefore if any man be in Christ, he is a new creature: old things are passed away; behold, all things are become new* (2 Corinthians 5:17).

Again, this is a choice we must make—but it's not just a one-time choice. We must choose every day, and really *anytime* we are given a choice, to live under the blessings of the covenant.

*And if it seem evil unto you to serve the Lord, choose you this day whom ye will serve; whether the gods which your fathers served that were on the other side of the flood, or the gods of the Amorites, in whose land ye dwell: but as for me and my house, we will serve the Lord* (Joshua 24:15).

Everything we've studied in this chapter points to the power God has put in Jesus' shed Blood. All of life is found in the Blood, and it has cleansed us from all sin and restored us to perfect fellowship with God. We are whole and complete in Him. We never could have done this for ourselves; we have new life only because of the powerful, life-giving Blood of Jesus!

# CHAPTER TWO

# THE COVENANT BLOOD

You, I, and all mankind have been on God's heart and mind for a long time! He was so committed to creating mankind. He wanted someone He could fellowship with. As we mentioned in the previous chapter, this would require that His very own Blood would have to be shed for the creation He would make in His own image. This was determined before the very foundation of the earth and mankind was given life.

From Genesis through Revelation, our God shows His desire to be in relationship with us. God knew man would eventually sin and the only way to get him back would be to redeem him through the Blood of Jesus Christ. How would He do this? He would enter a blood covenant with him. We see all throughout Scripture that the Lord is both a covenant-making and covenant-keeping God. He loves to keep His promises to His people. In fact, He can't *not* keep His promises. It is His very nature to be faithful and to do what He says!

This is why covenant is so important to the Lord. When we understand this and what defines the word *covenant*, it helps us to realize the importance of our blood covenant with God through Jesus Christ. The word *covenant* means "to cut." In Hebrew, the word is *berith* and refers to cutting two pieces of flesh and walking between those pieces (Strong's #H1285). This is how covenant was established. The root word is *bara*, meaning "to shape, create, or cut" (Strong's #H1254).

In Greek, the word is *diathéké* and refers to a will or a legal testament (Strong's #G1242). The act of making a covenant is a declaration of promise and agreement, but it is also a legally binding contract between two parties.

The very first blood covenant God made was with Abraham, and its purpose was to bring restoration of everything Adam had lost in the fall.

This first covenant was a foreshadowing of Jesus' Blood covenant that would destroy every work of the enemy, including sickness, death, disease, torment, and every affliction—completely restoring us to the Father.

> *Therefore know that the Lord your God, He is God, the faithful God who keeps covenant and mercy for a thousand generations with those*

*who love Him and keep His commandments* (Deuteronomy 7:9 NKJV).

*For this purpose the Son of God was manifested, that he might destroy the works of the devil* (1 John 3:8b).

We see a beautiful picture of what covenant is demonstrated now in the covenant between God and Abraham. We find that God could find no one greater than Himself to hold Him to His promises, so He swore by Himself (see Heb. 6:13). Thus holding Himself in honor to keep His word and keep His covenant promises to Abraham. In this blood covenant that was established between Abraham and God, we see the cutting of two pieces of flesh.

*And he said, Lord God, whereby shall I know that I shall inherit it? And he said unto him, Take me an heifer of three years old, and a she goat of three years old, and a ram of three years old, and a turtledove, and a young pigeon. And he took unto him all these, and divided them in the midst, and laid each piece one against another: but the birds divided he not* (Genesis 15:8-10).

The dividing of these carcasses would be what Abraham would be required to do to uphold his end of the covenant. This is also why Jesus had to shed His Blood on our behalf as it was required in the establishing of a true Blood covenant. The cutting of the flesh in two pieces is prophetically revealed in the bloody crucifixion of our Lord and

Savior Jesus Christ. Have you ever thought of why both His hands and feet were nailed and His Blood flowed from them? It was the signifying of the Blood covenant between God and mankind.

Another great truth to discover regarding the covenant of cutting in two is the blessings for those who kept the covenant and the curses or negative results of breaking it. How is that, you might ask? It is revealed in the two halves that Abraham divided, which we later find in powerful prophetic parallels in Scripture. For example, there were two mountains that the people of Israel came to understand in terms of one signifying the blessings, while the other signified the curse of not upholding the covenant. These two mountains were Mount Gerizim, where the blessing was spoken, and Mount Ebal, where they spoke the curse. It is important to mention that Mount Gerizim was lush and fertile while Mount Ebal was rocky and barren, clearly portraying the ramifications of our choices (see Deut. 27).

The blessings of the covenant and the negative results or the curses of not upholding the covenant are powerfully revealed to us in the crucifixion of our Lord Jesus and the two thieves hanging on each side of our Lord. One to His right and the other to His left symbolized the two halves in the cutting of covenant with Abraham, and the two mountains with Moses and the children of Israel. Notice, with the two criminals crucified with our Lord, that it was one of the thieves who received the blessing and blessed the Lord by asking Jesus to remember him when He entered paradise. It was the other thief being crucified with our

Lord who received the curse of eternal damnation by hurling insults at Him.

## The Importance of Two

This concept of "two"—as we have discovered in the two halves of Abraham, the two mountains of Gerizim and Ebal, as well as the two thieves—is repeated over and over in other examples throughout Scripture. Two is the number of covenant and it also indicates the need to make a choice. God is very intent on demonstrating His covenant with His people. Think about some instances where we see "two" in the Bible:

- God made covenant with Abram by passing between two pieces of flesh;
- Moses instructed the Israelites to stand on two mountains (Mount Ebal and Mount Gerizim) to pronounce blessings and curses;
- Moses carried two tablets down the mountain after meeting with God;
- The Red Sea parted in two;
- God led the Israelites with two pillars—the cloud by day and fire by night;
- Jesus was crucified between two thieves;
- Jesus talks of two types of nations at the end of the age—the sheep and the goats.

These are just some of the powerful signs God uses to reveal His commitment to us and encourage us to choose to live under the blessings of our Blood covenant with Jesus!

This is why we are told in Scripture that life and death is a part of the world we live in. Every day, we choose blessings or choose the curse of sinful things. Yet we are told by God in our covenant to always choose life and the way of blessings!

> *I call heaven and earth to record this day against you, that I have set before you life and death, blessing and cursing: therefore choose life, that both thou and thy seed may live* (Deuteronomy 30:19).

This choice of life or the blessing, as we see in this verse in Deuteronomy, was our upholding of the covenant before almighty God. Our choice would not just affect us but also those in our families.

Our choice to uphold the blessings of covenant living is a way of life for the believer. We also see this as God led the Israelites through the wilderness—the sign of covenant never left them. They were to continually live in the blessings of their covenant and avoid the negative results of ignoring it or, worse yet, rebelling against it. They were continually in the presence of a cloud by day and a fire by night. Even so, we know that many of them grew discontent and forgot their covenant; they perceived God's leading them through the wilderness as abandonment.

Like them, we can also grow weary when we feel like God has left us in the wilderness. However, no matter what, we must always choose to live and remind God of His faithful blessings He has provided and promised in our covenant with Him. Remember, He's promised to never leave us! If we look closely, we can always find signs of His eternal covenant with us.

> *Now when Pharaoh had let the people go, God did not lead them by the way of the land of the Philistines, even though it was near; for God said, "The people might change their minds when they see war, and return to Egypt." Hence God led the people around by the way of the wilderness to the Red Sea; and the sons of Israel went up in martial array from the land of Egypt.*
>
> *...The Lord was going before them in a pillar of cloud by day to lead them on the way, and in a pillar of fire by night to give them light, that they might travel by day and by night. He did not take away the pillar of cloud by day, nor the pillar of fire by night, from before the people* (Exodus 13:17-18, 21-22 NASB).

God provided the sign of the covenant in the pillar of cloud by day and the pillar of fire by night. These two pillars allowed the Israelites to travel both day and night. They were more than just signs of God's faithfulness—they were protection for the people. The Israelites did not have to fear because they were under the protection of the covenant! They should have known this as the cloud by day and the pillar by night were a prophetic reminder and symbol of the covenant God made with Abraham. It was a beautiful picture of the two halves of the bull cut in two by Abraham and the smoking furnace and the burning lamp carried by God Himself, establishing His covenant.

> *And it came to pass, that, when the sun went down, and it was dark, behold a smoking furnace, and a burning lamp that passed between those pieces. In the same day the Lord made a covenant with Abram, saying, Unto thy seed have I given this land, from the river of Egypt unto the great river, the river Euphrates* (Genesis 15:17-18).

Now the problem was, of course, we know that the children of Israel didn't see it that way!

> *For it would have been better for us to serve the Egyptians than to die in the wilderness* (Exodus 14:12b MEV).

The way God led them to the Red Sea was "by way of the wilderness." Our journey under God's covenant can sometimes look like the wilderness, and we may find ourselves crying out like the children of Israel, thinking He will let us die there. Remember, what looked like abandonment to them was actually God's protection of them: "*for God said, 'The people might change their minds when they see war, and return to Egypt'*" (Exodus 13:17 NASB). The wilderness is never the end of our story when we are in covenant with God!

When the children of Israel approached the Red Sea, Scripture tells us they were *"very frightened"* (see

Exod. 14:10 NASB) as the Egyptian army was chasing them. What a vivid picture of how the devil threatens to kill God's people. But look how Moses stood on the promises of his covenant-keeping God:

> *But Moses said to the people, "Do not fear! Stand by and see the salvation of the Lord which He will accomplish for you today; for the Egyptians whom you have seen today, you will never see them again forever. The Lord will fight for you while you keep silent"* (Exodus 14:13-14 NASB).

When the children of Israel were on their way into the sea, Moses told them to *"stand by"* (take their stand) and see what the Lord would accomplish. Notice Moses didn't tell them that *they* would accomplish their deliverance. They were only to *stand* under God's covenant promises, and they would be delivered as a result of His faithfulness to His Word!

As they passed through the Red Sea, the Israelites had a wall of water on their right and a wall of water on their left. Notice that they passed through the *Red* Sea. Red represents blood. The children of Israel passed through safely, and then the *Red Sea* engulfed and drowned their enemies. This passing through the Red Sea is God's blood covenant with Abraham in action. Abraham's covenant is our covenant. I believe that just as God passed between the pieces of flesh when He made covenant with Abram (whose name He changed to Abraham), God the Father and God the Son walked through the Red Sea with the children of

Israel to show them He was honoring that covenant for their benefit.

As we mentioned, the pillar of cloud by day prophetically revealed the burning smoke of God establishing the covenant with Abraham in Genesis 15. Yet it doesn't stop there! The fire by night that followed the children of Israel is revealed in the burning lamp that walked through the two halves of the bullock for Abraham! Just think—it was God Himself walking through the Red Sea as the pillar of cloud by day and the fire by night with Moses and the children of Israel, and it was the Father and the Son as the smoking furnace and burning lamp with Abraham.

We see this smoking furnace and pillar of cloud again when God visited Israel upon Mount Sinai in a cloud and smoke. The pillar of fire by night and the burning lamp also represent Jesus, as the book of Revelation reveals Him with eyes as a flame of fire and the glory of the Lamb of God that lights the heaven and the earth.

The power of our covenant with God is evident in God's deliverance that day against Pharaoh and his army at the parting of the Red Sea, as well as in the cloud by day and the pillar of fire by night. This is because His Blood always makes a way for us, and His Blood defeats our enemies! Israel had God Himself with them through every challenge and seemingly impossible situation as the cloud by day and the fire by night followed them. This is also a reminder that through our Blood covenant in Jesus Christ we have the overshadowing presence of God and His wonderful fire of protection and guidance. Whatever we need or whatever enemy we face, our covenant provides a way of blessing and the defeat of the enemy.

This is why we should never view stories in the Old Testament as just stories. No, they are written for our examples (see 1 Cor. 10). This is because everything we see in the Old Testament points to our New Testament promises, and the Israelites passing through the Red Sea points directly to the promises of Calvary. When Jesus was crucified, He hung between *two* thieves, and in the middle was a *Red Sea*, as Jesus was perfectly positioned to shed His very own Blood. This "Red Sea" saves us from our enemy in much the same way the children of Israel were saved from Pharaoh's army. In our day, the enemy chases God's people with oppression, financial troubles, disease, and a host of other issues, but we are offered perfect protection when we choose to walk through the "Red Sea" of Jesus' Blood covenant with us!

## When Two Become One

The institution of marriage is the most intimate covenant a man and a woman can make and is another way God demonstrates the power of covenant to us. The enemy has fought hard to defile the marriage covenant in our day, and it's crucial that we have a deep understanding of the covenant established through marriage. When a couple gets married, they symbolize their covenant by wearing wedding rings. Historically, the act of circumcision was also a physical sign of a "ring," meaning a man was in covenant with

God. When one man (circumcised with the ring) and one woman would consummate their marriage, there would be a shedding of blood. Again, we have a symbolic act representing God's covenant with us through Jesus' shed Blood.

God has declared that in marriage, two become one.

> *For this cause shall a man leave his father and mother, and shall be joined unto his wife, and they two shall be one flesh. This is a great mystery: but I speak concerning Christ and the church* (Ephesians 5:31-32).

What a powerful, beautiful demonstration of God's love for us and His desire that we enter into, and remain in, covenant with Him.

## WE MUST CHOOSE

Although God provides countless blessings for us under His covenant, they do not all automatically manifest in our lives every day. While the number *two* represents a covenant, it also represents choice or agreement. Whatever we choose, whether good or bad, we are agreeing with. As believers in Jesus Christ and His shed Blood, we must choose to live in the place of blessing and life as we mentioned earlier in this chapter, and we must make this choice *daily!* The devil and the Lord both work by agreement. What are we agreeing with, the blessing or the curse?

We will discuss this more in a later chapter, but let's look at how life and death are evident in our day-to-day lives. Life and blessing can look like abundance, prosperity, protection, health, long life for us and our children, land to possess—the *shalom* of God (see Deut. 28:1-12; John 10:10). Death and cursing might look like sickness, disease, anxiety, fear, addiction, oppression, heartache, or lack (see Deut. 28:13-46).

In our world today, think of how often God gets blamed for things like disease, car accidents, hurricanes, and other disasters. These things are not of God—they are the results of the curse or the works of the devil. He is a liar and a thief, and he will never change. He tries to attack our kids, our jobs, our finances, our health, our peace. He doesn't fight fair! But we must remember who he is and what he does so that we are careful not to blame the Lord for things the enemy brings about.

In John 10, Jesus clearly shows us two different ways of living. There is the way of the enemy who comes to steal, kill, and destroy; and there's the way of the blessed and abundant life Jesus has made available to us through His shed Blood (see John 10:10). This abundant life is provided by our blood covenant with Him!

Jesus is indeed the One who *"is able to do exceeding abundantly above all that we ask or think, according to the power that worketh in us"* (Eph. 3:20). I'm not saying we don't have trouble in this world. Jesus made it clear that we will all experience tribulation (see John 16:33), but He takes us *through* trials—we are not confined *to* them!

> *When thou passest through the waters, I will be with thee; and through the rivers, they shall not overflow thee* (Isaiah 43:2a).

Because He has overcome the world, we are made more than conquerors!

> *Who shall separate us from the love of Christ? Shall tribulation, or distress, or persecution, or famine, or nakedness, or peril, or sword? As it is written: "For Your sake we are killed all day long; we are accounted as sheep for the slaughter." Yet in all these things we are more than conquerors through Him who loved us* (Romans 8:35-37 NKJV).

As a result of what was accomplished at Calvary, we can have good health, great marriages, children who live in the blessing of God, and favor in our workplaces. We can live under the blessing and not under the curse, because Christ *has redeemed* us!

> *Christ has redeemed us from the curse of the law by being made a curse for us—as it is written, "Cursed is everyone who hangs on a tree"— so that the blessing of Abraham might come on the Gentiles through Jesus Christ, that we might receive the promise of the Spirit through faith* (Galatians 3:13-14 MEV).

Jesus shed His Blood *so that* He could link all people in every generation to the blessings of Abraham. This is why Paul tells the Galatians in this verse that it has also come upon the Gentiles. This is because, prior to that, the Jews were the only people who had access to God's covenant blessings. The covenant did not apply to non-Jews. But because of His great love for us, God made a way for *all* people to enter into His covenant and receive its blessings. At Calvary, the new covenant became available to all Gentiles (non-Jews) as well. Paul tells the Ephesians the truth of their condition before being brought under the new covenant—they were "apart, alienated, strangers, without hope, without God."

> *Therefore remember that formerly you, the Gentiles in the flesh, who are called the "uncircumcision" by the so-called "circumcision" in the flesh by human hands, were at that time apart from Christ, alienated from the citizenship of Israel and strangers to the covenants of promise, without hope and without God in the world. But now in Christ Jesus you who were formerly far away have been brought near by the blood of Christ* (Ephesians 2:11-13 MEV).

Everyone who chooses to live under the new covenant is a child of Abraham, and in him all the nations of the earth shall be blessed. This means you and me! It is the abundant life that Jesus was speaking of and the blessings that He spoke to Abraham that are now ours as believers.

> *You are the sons of the prophets and of the covenant which God made with our fathers, saying to Abraham, "And in your seed shall all the families of the earth be blessed"* (Acts 3:25 MEV).

Look at God's wonderful promise to Abraham and now to us through our covenant with Jesus Christ:

> *And I will make of you a great nation, and I will bless you [with abundant increase of favors] and make your name famous and distinguished, and you will be a blessing [dispensing good to others]* (Genesis 12:2 AMPC).

## CHOOSING LIFE

This is the God-kind of life that Jesus was speaking of in John 10, which is now available to us in our covenant with Him! How do we choose life? Some of the ways we can choose life are by saying no to things of the world; by making choices about what we watch, what we listen to, how we treat others, and the words we speak.

Let's look at how powerful our words can be: *"Death and life are in the power of the tongue, and they that love it shall eat the fruit thereof"* (Prov. 18:21). This choice of death or life sounds a lot like the two mountains we spoke of in this chapter and the two criminals crucified with Jesus. Again, when the two robbers were crucified with Jesus, one chose death and cursing, but the second chose life and blessing, both by their words!

> *Then one of the criminals who were hanged blasphemed Him, saying, "If You are the Christ, save Yourself and us"* (Luke 23:39 NKJV).

Does that sound familiar? Do you remember when the devil tempted Jesus in the wilderness in Luke 4? Several times his words were, "If You are the Christ." This thief on the cross was literally repeating the devil's words to Jesus.

But look at what the second thief says in response as he speaks words of life:

> *But the other, answering, rebuked him, saying, "Do you not even fear God, seeing you are under the same condemnation? And we indeed justly, for we receive the due reward of our deeds; but this Man has done nothing wrong." Then he said to Jesus, "Lord, remember me when You come into Your kingdom"* (Luke 23:40-42 NKJV).

And the best part of all, look at Jesus' response to the man who spoke words of life:

> *And Jesus said to him, "Assuredly, I say to you, today you will be with Me in Paradise"* (Luke 23:43 NKJV).

By *speaking* one thief chose death and the other chose life. Our words are powerful, just like the words of this man who chose the way of life over death and the blessing over the curse!

James reminds us of the power of our words and that the same mouth that speaks words of life can also speak words of death:

> *We all err in many ways. But if any man does not err in word, he is a perfect man and able also to control the whole body. See how we put bits in*

*the mouths of horses that they may obey us, and we control their whole bodies. And observe ships. Though they are so great and are driven by fierce winds, yet they are directed with a very small rudder wherever the captain pleases. Even so, the tongue is a little part of the body and boasts great things* (James 3:2-5a MEV).

*With it we bless the Lord and Father, and with it we curse men, who are made in the image of God. Out of the same mouth proceed blessing and cursing. My brothers, these things ought not to be so* (James 3:9-10 MEV).

There is protection and blessing not only in our mouths but also how we activate our covenant rights and privileges. We see this in Psalm 91, as it encourages us to abide under the shadow of the Lord's wings and reminds of the wonderful protection provided for us as we choose to remain close to Him. This is no small matter—we solidify our choices with the words we speak, so let's speak life and stay in our perfect place of protection! It is our legal right of being in covenant with almighty God through accepting Him as our Lord and Savior.

## OUR LEGAL RIGHTS

When we are born again, we become legal recipients of all the benefits of Jesus' Blood covenant. Jesus is called our Mediator, our Intercessor, and our Advocate (or Attorney). Why does Scripture use legal terms to describe Him? It is because our Blood covenant with Him is both a promise and a legal transaction that entitles us to every benefit His Blood provides.

As we discussed earlier, it is not enough for us to only have head knowledge of what Jesus provided for us when He shed His Blood. In order to live in the blessings Jesus died to give us, we must understand how to use the rights to this shed Blood. It is our legal right to actively use Jesus' Blood and experience all the benefits it provides!

We can have money in the bank, but if we never make a withdrawal, it doesn't do us much good. We could literally be millionaires and still live in lack if we fail to use the money that is rightfully ours. In the same way, we are to declare our legal right to all the benefits of Jesus' shed Blood and apply them to our lives and the lives of our loved ones. We'll discuss how to do this in more detail in a later chapter.

We know that Jesus had to shed His Blood, because without the shedding of blood there is no remission of sins (see Heb. 9:22). The fountain of Jesus' Blood was opened when He shed it for us and gave us legal right and access to all the promises of our covenant with Him (see Zech. 13:1). This Blood right *is* continually and eternally available to us. Did you notice it's not a drop of blood or a little bit of blood? It's a *fountain* that is continually flowing toward children of the covenant. This fountain contains all the Blood rights, privileges, and benefits that Jesus gave us when He died on the cross. We are to exercise our rights *daily* and not forget what He has done for us!

This is exactly what David told us in Psalm 103 regarding our covenant benefits. We are to remember them by claiming them and rehearsing them before the Lord.

> *Bless the Lord, O my soul: and all that is within me, bless his holy name. Bless the Lord, O my soul, and forget not all his benefits: who forgiveth all thine iniquities; who healeth all thy diseases; who redeemeth thy life from destruction; who crowneth thee with lovingkindness and tender mercies; who satisfieth thy mouth with good things; so that thy youth is renewed like the eagle's. The Lord executeth righteousness and judgment for all that are oppressed* (Psalm 103:1-6).

Now, what exactly are we calling on when we call on the Blood of Jesus? These verses in Psalms give a great description of what the Lord has provided for us and instruct us to *"forget not all His benefits."* I encourage you to read these slowly and meditate on what Scripture is *really* saying. We often read certain passages quickly when we are familiar with them and don't absorb their meaning. Because Scripture is "living and active" (see Heb. 4:12), it can reveal things to us that we may have never seen, regardless of how many times we may have read it before!

Our covenant-keeping God has provided these covenant benefits as mentioned in Psalm 103. Look at all the blessings that have been provided through His shed blood for us!

- Forgives all our sins
- Heals all our diseases
- Redeems our lives from destruction
- Crowns us with lovingkindness and tender mercies
- Satisfies our mouths with good things
- Renews our youth like the eagle's
- Executes righteousness and justice for all who are oppressed
- Makes His ways known
- Is great in mercy
- Makes us His children
- Is ruler of all

These wonderful benefits are given to us today because we have a High Priest (Jesus). We are invited to come *boldly* to the throne and receive grace, mercy, and help in time of need (see Heb. 4:16). Did you notice that when we approach His throne, we already receive or obtain the promises of grace, mercy, and the Lord's help and we don't have to ask for them? This is because the fountain of His Blood and our Blood rights are available to all who come to the Father through our covenant with Jesus Christ. We are invited because Jesus' Blood gives us a legal right to be there, and also a legal right to receive His grace, mercy, and help in the time of our need. Just like as we read with Israel as they walked through the Red Sea, His grace, mercy, and help was available to them in their time of need. It is the same today for us through the Blood of Jesus. The Blood rights He provided are our way out of trouble, like with Israel. It is always through the "Red Sea"—His Blood!

## How Is This Possible?

Scripture tells us that Jesus was legally established as our eternal Mediator because of His Blood. Hebrews 9 tells us the power of Jesus' Blood in cleansing us from our sins and establishing His everlasting covenant.

> *Neither by the blood of goats and calves, but by His own blood, He entered the Most Holy Place once for all, having obtained eternal redemption. For if the blood of bulls and goats, and the ashes of a heifer, sprinkling the unclean, sanctifies so that the flesh is purified, how much more shall the blood of Christ, who through the eternal Spirit offered Himself without blemish to God, cleanse your conscience from dead works to serve the living God? For this reason He is the Mediator of a new covenant, since a death has occurred for the redemption of the sins that were committed under the first covenant, so that those who are called might receive the promise of eternal inheritance* (Hebrews 9:12-15 MEV).

Jesus' throne is now eternal—it will never end! From His throne He is positioned as our Intercessor, standing in the gap between us and the judgment we deserve. He stands between, holding the Blood rights of His children!

As our Mediator, Intercessor, and Advocate, He relates perfectly to those He represents.

> *For we have not an high priest which cannot be touched with the feeling of our infirmities; but was in all points tempted like as we are, yet without sin* (Hebrews 4:15).

Because our perfect High Priest established His eternal Blood covenant with us, we can come boldly to the throne of grace, not just once, but whenever we need to! It is the throne of *grace*; we will always find grace, mercy, and help here in our time of need (see Heb. 4:16).

Legally speaking, Jesus is the One perfectly positioned between us and any judgment that would be rendered. His Blood is our defense against every accusation of the enemy, and His Blood declares us *not guilty!* It is why it is so important we remember our covenant rights, which Jesus provided and paid for with His own Blood.

## REMEMBERING COVENANT

> *So God heard their groaning and God remembered His covenant with Abraham, Isaac, and Jacob (Israel). God saw the sons of Israel, and God took notice [of them] and was concerned about them [knowing all, understanding all, remembering all]* (Exodus 2:24-25 AMP).

When the Israelites cried out to God in their bondage, He moved on their behalf. He didn't just move because of their groaning; He moved when He remembered His covenant! The people of Israel spent over four hundred years in bondage, and it doesn't mention that they remembered the covenant, but it was God who chose to remember through His mercy. It is why we can't allow life to get us down or hold us in bondage, thus leading to us forgetting our covenant benefits. We need to remind God of His covenant. This is why prayer and rehearsing our covenant rights and benefits are vital. There is something special that happens in the heart of the Father when we remind Him of His promises. Remember, it is why David said in Psalm 103, "Don't forget His benefits!" It's not presumptuous to remind Him of His Word or the covenant we have with Him—in fact, He always responds to His Word (see Isa. 55:11). It is our legal right and our benefit as His children to remind Him of His covenant, but it doesn't stop there. It is also as serious and important as when a husband and wife exchange their wedding vows, promising to walk in agreement in their marriage. It is not just to be upheld at the time of the wedding only but throughout their marriage.

When a couple gets married, there is great anticipation of the wedding day. But if their relationship and commitment to each other ended there, what kind of marriage relationship would they have? God's intent in making covenant with us is not that it would be a one-day, one-time event, but that just as couples live and grow together in marriage, our covenant with Him would be strengthened through the years we spend in relationship with Him. Beyond being our legal right, reminding God of His covenant strengthens our bond with Him. As we put more and more trust in Him, we experience more and more of His faithfulness. Remember, God is not only a covenant-making God; He is a covenant-keeping God. He's not just here for the wedding day; He wants to enjoy the entire marriage! Reminding God of His covenant is part of living in constant communication and intimacy with Him. We are the bride of Christ, and this is one of the most beautiful aspects of our relationship!

We must always remember the importance of our relationship and covenant with God. It is likened to the seriousness of a marriage between a man and a woman who love God together. We are to rest in the assurance that not only will the husband and wife uphold their covenant with each other but with God at the center. An example of upholding the covenant is Abram (Abraham). He knew the implication of a blood covenant, so when God promised him all the land from the river of Egypt to the Euphrates, he asked, "O Sovereign Lord, how can I know that I will gain possession of it?" (see Gen. 15:8). Abram was looking for additional assurance from God that he would gain possession of the land. Basically, he was asking God to make a binding covenant with him, and that is what God did:

> *On that day the Lord made a covenant with Abram and said, "To your descendants I give this land, from the Wadi of Egypt to the great river, the Euphrates"* (Genesis 15:18 NIV).

The Hebrew writer comments on this passage and says:

*God, desiring even more to show to the heirs of the promise the unchangeableness of His purpose, interposed with an oath, so that by two unchangeable things in which it is impossible for God to lie, we who have taken refuge would have strong encouragement to take hold of the hope set before us* (Hebrews 6:17b-18 NASB).

We can see from this verse that there are two things God cannot do: He cannot lie, and He cannot go back on His covenant. This gave Abram assurance that he had both God's promise and the covenant to confirm that promise. There is nothing more certain in the universe or in all of eternity than God's covenant. He will always keep His covenant with us! We then must do our part to honor it and keep it as well.

When the Lord called Moses up to Mount Sinai, He told him that if Israel obeyed His voice and kept His covenant, they would be a peculiar treasure to Him. In other words, if they would keep their end of the agreement, they would hold a place in His heart but also would delight in His blessings. It is always a choice for us to remember our covenant with God.

Just as God remembers to keep His part of the covenant, we will be His treasure if we live out our part, obeying Him and choosing life by the words we speak and decisions we make. Covenant is very important to God, and there is an abundant life promised for those who live in that covenant and make it a regular practice to remind Him of it!

*Now therefore, if ye will obey my voice indeed, and keep my covenant, then ye shall be a peculiar treasure unto me above all people: for all the earth is mine* (Exodus 19:5).

# CHAPTER THREE

# THE OVERCOMING BLOOD

The Bible is full of amazing stories of real-life people like you and me, not fables. I've always loved these stories of *overcomers*—people who put all their trust in God and were protected and rescued out of some of the most extreme situations. Think of heroes like Noah, Moses, Joshua, Gideon, Daniel, David, and Apostle Paul to name just a few. They are the some of the ones mentioned in Revelation, who *"overcame him by the blood of the Lamb, and by the word of their testimony; and they loved not their lives unto the death"* (Rev. 12:11). Ultimately, these heroes overcame because they were trusting in the God of the blood covenant!

I want to highlight a few stories that show us powerful physical representations of the blood covenant at work on behalf of God's people. These stories are to show us that we too can and will overcome any obstacle if we understand the power of our covenant with God through Jesus Christ. Let's look at how the Lord demonstrated His covenant to the Israelites at the Red Sea, the River Jordan, and through the battle between David and Goliath.

## THE RED SEA CROSSING

There are several powerful ways that the Lord demonstrated His covenant to the children of Israel during the Passover and the Red Sea crossing. He began by showing the enforcing of His covenant of blood at the Passover, which was a picture of salvation and the rights of their covenant through the lamb's blood. How is that, you might ask? They were saved, delivered, healed, and protected when they applied the blood of the lamb upon the doorposts (see Exod. 12). In the same way, when we open the door of our hearts we are cleansed by the Blood of the Lamb of God, Jesus Christ, and we are saved and forgiven of our sins. We too, like Israel on the night of the Passover, are given blood rights because of the Lamb's Blood, Jesus Christ's, which was shed. If that is not enough, we also are saved and even healed, as we see when the Scripture mentions that there was not one feeble among them (see Ps. 105:37). In addition, we too are protected, delivered, and rescued from harm just as they were. These are all the rights and benefits of our covenant that come at the time of our salvation. It is not just salvation but a salvation package!

As the Scripture says, this happens when you call upon the name of the Lord at the time of salvation!

> *Whoever calls on the name of the Lord shall be saved* (Romans 10:13 NKJV).

It is at this time that you receive your covenant birth rights when you call upon the Lord to be saved. However, this word *saved* means more than just salvation. It is revealing our salvation package given at the time of our new birth in Christ. The word *saved* in this verse in Romans 10 is the Greek word *sozo* or *sodezo* (Strong's #4982). It contains three contexts: salvation, healing, and deliverance. These are all part of your spiritual new birthright of your covenant with God! This word has such rich meaning and definition. This word *saved,* or *sozo,* means "to save; to make whole or well; to save, deliver, heal, preserve, provide; keep safe and sound; rescue from danger or destruction, from injury or peril; to restore health; to heal." This is so important to know what we truly receive when we are saved so we can fully understand what is truly made available to us at the time of our salvation. As we said in the previous chapter, we are remembering our covenant rights and putting God in remembrance as well.

We must know and claim our *sozo* rights because what we receive is more than just salvation, forgiveness of sins, eternal life, and a mansion in heaven. It is so much more! The problem is many only receive or are aware of salvation (*sozo*) saving them from their sins. Sadly, for most people this is where the power of *sozo*, or salvation, stops. They often think that the only thing that is received upon asking Jesus into their heart is salvation, not realizing the "full package" of *sozo* rights. Again, it is important to understand that we don't just receive forgiveness of sin, salvation, and the promise of eternal life, but all the things that this word means, which Jesus paid for in full through His shed blood! You get so much more. Remember, those who call on the name of the Lord shall be saved; shall be made whole or well; shall be delivered, healed, preserved, provided for, kept safe and sound; shall be rescued from danger or destruction, from injury or peril; and shall be restored to health.

These are amazing covenant benefits given through Jesus' shed Blood, which we received when we were saved, and also prophetically foreshadowed the night of the Passover with the children of Israel. It doesn't stop there, as we continue to see these covenant rights enforced and revealed in Israel's journey leading them to the Red Sea crossing.

Following the Passover and their deliverance from Egypt, the children of Israel would pass through the Red Sea, which is a picture of baptism and God honoring His covenant promises with them. First Corinthians 10:2 tells us, *"And were all baptized unto Moses in the cloud and in the sea."*

This once again enforced the covenant that God made with Abraham, but they didn't see it as that. It should have been revealed to them, as they saw the sea open upon their right and upon their left, that this was a powerful reminder of the two halves of the bull that Abraham cut as he entered into covenant with God. Instead of seeing their covenant in this powerful display of God's might, they got into fear. We too often do as Israel did. Instead of reminding God of our covenant with Him and our powerful rights of healing, deliverance, protection, and rescue, to name a few, we get into fear and doubt.

At the Red Sea, God was displaying the power and rights of their covenant, especially as they passed through the sea. They saw the Lord defeat their enemies and use those same enemies to provide the weapons they'd need for future battles. This means not only does our covenant defeat our enemies, but it is a weapon against them!

The Lord had already provided the Israelites with silver, gold, and the riches of the Egyptians as they'd left Egypt (see Exod. 12:35-36). God had made sure they were well-supplied with the resources to eventually build their own economy. While they left Egypt with these material goods, they'd been slaves and so they likely had no weapons of their own.

Scripture tells us that when the Israelites passed through the sea on dry land, they saw the bodies of the Egyptian soldiers on the shore.

*And the waters returned, and covered the chariots, and the horsemen, and all the host of Pharaoh that came into the sea after them; there remained not so much as one of them. But the children of Israel walked upon dry land in the midst of the sea; and the waters were a wall unto them on their right hand, and on their left. Thus the Lord saved Israel that day out of the hand of the Egyptians; and Israel saw the Egyptians dead upon the sea shore* (Exodus 14:28-30).

These Egyptian soldiers had been chasing the Israelites, so it's safe to assume they would have had their weapons strapped to them or in their hands. Now they were lying dead upon the shore with an entire army's worth of weapons! Through these dead soldiers, God provided His children with weapons for the battles they would encounter. In the same way, because of Jesus' Blood covenant, your enemy has been stripped of his power and you've been given weapons to fight!

Do you see how the Lord was already one step ahead of the children of Israel, and He was preparing them for what was to come? What a great reminder that God will always give us what we need to win any battle we might encounter, whether now or in the future, because of our covenant rights and benefits.

The Israelites were well supplied with the spoils of the Egyptians and their battle weapons. In the same way, under Jesus' Blood covenant, the Lord will always supply our material needs and give us weapons to fight and to win the battles we face! As they crossed the Red Sea, the children of Israel crossed over from slavery to victory. This is true for us—when you are baptized in the name of Jesus, you cross over into the victory of His Blood covenant!

## The Crossing of the River Jordan

*And as they that bare the ark were come unto Jordan, and the feet of the priests that bare the ark were dipped in the brim of the water, (for Jordan overfloweth all his banks all the time of harvest,) that the waters which came down from above stood and rose up upon an heap very far from the city Adam, that is beside Zaretan: and those that came down toward the sea of the plain, even the salt sea, failed, and were cut off: and the people passed over right against Jericho. And the priests that bare the ark of the covenant of the Lord stood firm on dry ground in the midst of Jordan, and all the Israelites passed over on dry ground, until all the people were passed clean over Jordan* (Joshua 3:15-17).

Much like what happened when the Israelites crossed the Red Sea, Joshua led the people through the Jordan River and saw their enemies drowned. Immediately following this, the Lord instructed Joshua to circumcise the Israelites to prepare them for battle (see Josh. 5).

The children of Israel had been in the wilderness for forty years but had never circumcised their male children during that time. This was an act of rebellion on the Israelites' part. They knew the significance of circumcision, and they knew the statement they were making by not doing it. Essentially, they were saying, "We don't want to honor our covenant that God made with our forefathers, and we don't need the Lord!" As a result of ignoring or rebelling against their covenant with God, many of them died in the wilderness, and their children were removed from under the promise and protection of covenant!

> *For the children of Israel walked forty years in the wilderness, till all the people that were men of war, which came out of Egypt, were consumed, because they obeyed not the voice of the Lord: unto whom the Lord sware that he would not shew them the land, which the Lord sware unto their fathers that he would give us, a land that floweth with milk and honey* (Joshua 5:6).

The original generation had been circumcised (a sign of the covenant) prior to entering the wilderness. In fact, the sign of covenant was there as a reminder of the Lord's commitment to them to help bring them through those years in the desert. Unfortunately, they allowed the wilderness to harden their hearts and displayed their rebellion by not circumcising their sons.

> *And their children, whom he raised up in their stead, them Joshua circumcised: for they were uncircumcised, because they had not circumcised them by the way* (Joshua 5:7).

Thankfully, Joshua was obedient and performed the circumcision of a generation that would have otherwise been lost.

> *And the Lord said unto Joshua, This day have I rolled away the reproach of Egypt from off you. Wherefore the name of the place is called Gilgal unto this day* (Joshua 5:9).

When Joshua circumcised the Israelites again, he rescued a generation who'd been born into disobedience in the wilderness. Because Joshua understood the importance of covenant, he brought the next generation out of reproach and back into the victories and promises of the covenant.

Once they'd been circumcised, the Israelites were under covenant again, and covenant would be their defense and defeat their enemy. When they went into their next battle at Jericho, we know what a great victory they won.

Like the children of Israel who were grumbling and rebellious in the desert, there are many today who refuse to enter into covenant with God from their hearts. They look only at what they can see with natural eyes, and they often blame God for what is happening in their lives and the world. They choose ignorance or rebellion and they do not have the confidence of covenant to defeat their enemies. Instead, they themselves are defeated by the devil and his forces of darkness.

God's heart is that no one would live in lack, despair, and defeat. Out of His abundant mercy, He's provided every person with a wonderful opportunity to enter into covenant with Him from our hearts. When we do so, we are provided the overcoming Blood that enables us to defeat all our enemies!

## DAVID AND GOLIATH

David also knew the power of covenant and the character of the God he served. When he ran toward Goliath on the battlefield, he was putting all his trust in his covenant-keeping God! When all the men of Israel ran away in fear, David was so confident in God's covenant with him that he ran *toward* the giant (see 1 Sam. 17:48).

Remember what David asked before the battle:

> *And David spake to the men that stood by him, saying, What shall be done to the man that killeth this Philistine, and taketh away the reproach from Israel? for who is this uncircumcised Philistine, that he should defy the armies of the living God?* (1 Samuel 17:26).
>
> *Then said David to the Philistine, Thou comest to me with a sword, and with a spear, and with a shield: but I come to thee in the name of the Lord of hosts, the God of the armies of Israel, whom thou hast defied* (1 Samuel 17:45).

We know that circumcision was a sign of the covenant. David was saying, "Goliath has no covenant, but I do!" He knew he was a son under the covenant, and he also knew Goliath's defeat as a Philistine—one who lived outside of covenant with God.

David carried his five smooth stones to battle, and we often marvel at how Goliath fell so quickly when David threw that first stone. It's true that he'd practiced for years so he was very skilled, but I believe David won the battle that day because of a much bigger stone. Remember how the New Testament promises are revealed through the Old Testament? In Matthew 16, Jesus asked the disciples, "*Whom say ye that I am?*" Peter spoke the revelation he understood about Jesus: "*Thou art the Christ, the Son of the living God*" (Matt. 16:15-16).

> *And Jesus answered and said unto him, Blessed art thou, Simon Barjona: for flesh and blood hath not revealed it unto thee, but my Father which is in heaven* (Matthew 16:17).

Jesus confirmed that Peter's revelation had been given by the Father.

> *And I say also unto thee, That thou art Peter, and upon this rock I will build my church; and the gates of hell shall not prevail against it* (Matthew 16:18).

Did you see that? When Jesus said His church would be built "upon this rock," He was speaking of the revelation of Him as the Christ, the Anointed One, the Perfect Lamb of God—the One who made the eternal Blood covenant with us! It would be upon this revelation Peter received that the church would stand strong like a solid rock against the forces of darkness. All because of our blood covenant through Jesus Christ!

David had a similar revelation to Peter's, which would be a solid rock that would knock Goliath out. We see this as he ran unafraid toward Goliath, but he wasn't depending on five smooth stones to win the battle—he was trusting in the "rock" of the revelation of his covenant! He could trust in his gift of accurately throwing the stones because he was standing in his covenant with God. The giant fell and the gates of hell did not prevail against God's people that day!

Moses, Joshua, and David were not perfect men; Scripture doesn't hide their human nature from us. They won great victories because they each had an understanding of the God who keeps His Blood covenant promises. As they stepped out in faith, these three men saw their enemies defeated and ensured the children of Israel experienced the blessings of God's covenant with them.

Don't think for a moment that this same God of covenant won't rescue and protect you when you cry out to Him! As a born-again believer, Jesus' Blood covenant entitles you to tremendous victories in your life and the life of your family. When you put your confidence in the God of covenant, you can run toward every giant and watch them fall as you stand strong upon the revelation of the solid rock of your covenant with God!

## KNOW YOUR WEAPONS

It is important that you, like David, not only understand your covenant rights but also your mighty weapons available. Imagine you're a soldier and you're heading to the front lines for battle. You're tired, you're carrying over sixty pounds of gear, including your body armor and weapons for the fight. You can see the enemy coming, but you don't use your gun. What would happen? You'd probably have a pretty bad day, to say the least.

As believers, we sometimes don't want to acknowledge that we're in a battle or we avoid it all together. Fighting isn't always easy, and sometimes we get weary. We must never forget that we've been fully armed and equipped for every battle. Paul reminds us of three specific weapons we've been given in Second Corinthians 6:7:

- the Word of truth, referring to the Scriptures
- the power of God (We see this activated through the baptism of the Holy Spirit and praying in tongues.)
- the armor of righteousness (We are made righteous by the Blood of Jesus.)

*By the word of truth, by the power of God, by the armour of righteousness on the right hand and on the left* (2 Corinthians 6:7).

When we know the power of these weapons and become skillful in using them, we become a force to be reckoned with! Think about it—we have Jesus' very own Blood to use against the enemy. If we never make use of that Blood, calling on it, pleading it, hiding ourselves under it, we are like a soldier on the front lines who doesn't use their gun—we are really vulnerable to being hit by the forces of darkness. This is why Goliath couldn't harm David because of the powerful understanding and trust David had in the blood covenant with his God.

We certainly do live in a fallen world, and attacks will come, but the Blood is available to us at any moment, in any situation. It is the fountain that continually flows toward us (see Zech. 13:1). Remember, the Blood is one of our most powerful weapons, and God intends for us to use it!

> *Behold, I give unto you power to tread on serpents and scorpions, and over all the power of the enemy: and nothing shall by any means hurt you* (Luke 10:19).

## Know the Enemy

Just as we need to be skillful and know what belongs to us under Jesus' Blood covenant, we also need to know the tactics of our enemy. Knowing how the enemy operates is a major key in winning any battle. In our case, we know that our enemy doesn't rest. He *constantly prowls around seeking whom he can devour* (see 1 Pet. 5:8). We also know that he *comes to steal, kill, and destroy* (see John 10:10). He is a liar and the *accuser of the brethren* (see Rev. 12:10). He *disguises himself in light* (see 2 Cor. 11:14). To put it simply, everything the enemy does is an attempt to keep us from living in the fullness of our Blood covenant rights.

From the moment God made covenant with Abram, the enemy was there to try to interrupt and hinder everything God intended for His children.

> *Then Abram brought all of these to Him and cut them in two and laid each piece opposite the other, but he did not cut the birds in half. When the birds of prey came down on the carcasses, Abram drove them away* (Genesis 15:10-11 MEV).

In this passage of Genesis, these birds of prey do not serve the function of God; they serve another master. These birds are demons; they are birds from hell. Abram recognized what kind of birds these were and drove them away. We know that our enemy seeks to steal, kill, and destroy; he seeks "whom he may devour." We must be quick and decisive in driving these "birds of prey" away from our lives, our families, our health, etc. in the same way Abram drove them away! They come to challenge and hinder our covenant rights and privileges.

Throughout Scripture, fowls of the air are also associated with the curse (see Lev. 11:13-19; Deut. 28:26; Jer. 7:33; 1 Kings 14:11). In the Parable of the Sower, Jesus explained how the devil, through these "birds of the air," still tries to come to devour the Word (our covenant) when it is sown into our hearts.

> *Listen! And take note: A sower went out to sow. As he sowed, some seed fell beside the path, and the birds of the air came and devoured it* (Mark 4:3-4 MEV).
>
> *Then He said to them, "Do you not understand this parable? How then will you understand all*

*the parables? The sower sows the word. These are those beside the path, where the word is sown. But when they hear, Satan comes immediately and takes away the word which is sown in their hearts"* (Mark 4:13-15 MEV).

The seed that fell beside the path was devoured by the *"birds of the air."* *"Satan comes immediately and takes."* Again, here comes a devourer!

We still live in a world that is under the influence of the evil one. He will come and try to steal what is rightfully yours. When you see the enemy coming to steal your peace or trying to take your finances or trying to destroy your relationships, don't be passive! Be like Abram—get up and get close to the covenant. Chase away the devil and all his demons! Remember, you have infinitely more power than any "bird of the air" that wants to steal your promises. You have the power of Jesus' own Blood! It's your covenant right!

We are no different from the heroes in Scripture who overcame because they understood the power of Blood covenant and knew the faithfulness of their covenant-keeping God. Jesus' Blood has given us all that we need to defeat the enemy. When we're familiar with our enemy's strategies and we know the power of this covenant Blood, we can activate its protection for ourselves and our families and chase the devil away from every aspect of our lives!

# CHAPTER FOUR

# THE SHED BLOOD

We have come to understand the life-giving blood of Jesus, our covenant rights through His blood, and how we overcome by knowing our covenant. Now we will discover in this chapter more profound truths regarding the precious shed Blood of Jesus, the Lamb of God!

John the Baptist had the awesome privilege of announcing the start of Jesus' ministry on earth:

> *The next day John seeth Jesus coming unto him, and saith, Behold the Lamb of God, which taketh away the sin of the world* (John 1:29).

Notice that he didn't declare Jesus as Prophet or King but as "*the Lamb of God.*" Though he wouldn't live to see the sacrifice of this perfect Lamb, John the Baptist was a faithful voice who proclaimed both the arrival and the fulfillment of the Kingdom of God.

Three years later, as Jesus sat and ate His final Passover meal with His disciples, He explained the significance of His body and the Blood He was about to shed. It would contain all the promises and rights of this new covenant. They were about to behold the Lamb of God as *their* sacrificial Lamb, shedding the Blood that would take away the sin of the world.

> *Then He took the bread, and when He had given thanks, He broke it and gave it to them, saying, "This is My body which is given for you. Do this in remembrance of Me." In like manner, He took the cup after supper, saying, "This cup is the new covenant in My blood which is shed for you"* (Luke 22:19-20 MEV).

Notice in this verse Jesus mentions His Blood that would be shed for you and me! The emphasis was upon it being His shed Blood. This is vital to understand, as the Scriptures refer to both the shed Blood and the Blood of sprinkling. We will look at the clear distinction between *shed* Blood and *sprinkled* Blood in these next two chapters. As I mentioned, it's important that we understand these two different aspects of Jesus' Blood and what they mean for us as believers. The shed Blood *is* our covenant, and the sprinkled Blood is how we apply the benefits of this covenant to our lives.

All our victory and all our protection come from Jesus Himself—our perfect, spotless Lamb! At His last Passover meal, Jesus commanded His disciples to remember the covenant He was making with them through His body and His shed Blood. Let's look closer at the powerful picture of the first Passover, foreshadowing what Jesus would do for us on the cross.

## A Lamb, the Lamb, Your Lamb

Remember that the children of Israel were instructed to apply the blood of a shed lamb to their houses in order to provide protection.

> *Speak ye unto all the congregation of Israel, saying, In the tenth day of this month they shall take to them every man a lamb, according to the house of their fathers, a lamb for an house* (Exodus 12:3).

Did you see that? A lamb was required for every house. *A* lamb. But verse four gets a little more specific about this lamb. It goes from being *a* lamb to being *the* lamb.

> *And if the household be too little for the lamb, let him and his neighbour next unto his house take it according to the number of the souls; every man according to his eating shall make your count for the lamb* (Exodus 12:4).

Verse five gives the people ownership of this lamb by describing it as *your lamb.*

*Your lamb shall be without blemish, a male of the first year: ye shall take it out from the sheep, or from the goats* (Exodus 12:5).

There is a clear progression from *a lamb* to *the lamb* and then to *your lamb*. This is a beautiful prophetic description of Jesus: He is a Lamb, but more than that, He is *the* Lamb, and as He proved when He shed His Blood for you, He ultimately desires you to choose Him as your Lamb! It is not enough to hear how He came to die for all mankind as a Lamb, the Lamb of God who would take away the sins of the world, but we need to receive Him in our lives as our personal Savior and Lord. He must become our Lamb!

The Israelites took their own personal lamb into their homes. This lamb would be sacrificed in Exodus 12, and its shed blood, when applied as God instructed, would provide protection for all who were in the household. God had told them that when He passed through to smite the Egyptians, He would spare every house where He saw the blood had been applied to the sides and tops of the doors.

Let's look at that a little more closely. When the lamb's shed blood was applied to the top of the door and to both sides, it formed the shape of a cross. Here's another prophetic act that points directly to our new covenant with Jesus! In John 10:9, Jesus said:

*I am the door: by me if any man enter in, he shall be saved, and shall go in and out, and find pasture.*

At Calvary, the Blood of *the* Lamb (Jesus) was on *the* Door (Jesus), giving all who come through that Door the promise of eternal protection from sin and death!

In Hebrew culture, several generations would share the same household, so protection over a house meant that family's God-ordained destiny would be preserved from one generation to the next. It also was a beautiful picture of household salvation through the Blood! Once this shed blood from the lamb was applied, the blood was powerful and effective because through it God showed Himself faithful to the covenant He'd made with Abraham. Applying the blood to a house was a picture of complete protection; there are no holes in the blood.

> *And they shall take of the blood, and strike it on the two side posts and on the upper door post of the houses, wherein they shall eat it* (Exodus 12:7).
>
> *For I will pass through the land of Egypt this night, and will smite all the firstborn in the land of Egypt, both man and beast; and against all the gods of Egypt I will execute judgment: I am the Lord. And the blood shall be to you for a token upon the houses where ye are: and when I see the blood, I will pass over you, and the plague shall not be upon you to destroy you, when I smite the land of Egypt* (Exodus 12:12-13).
>
> *For the Lord will pass through to smite the Egyptians; and when he seeth the blood upon the*

*lintel, and on the two side posts, the Lord will pass over the door, and will not suffer the destroyer to come in unto your houses to smite you* (Exodus 12:23).

The two side-posts are also prophetic symbols of the two halves of the animals God passed between when He made covenant with Abram. Remember, *two* is necessary for establishing covenant. Applying the blood to the upper doorpost represents authority *over* the devil. Notice that the blood was not to be applied anywhere on the floor or the ground, because it is sacred and not to be trampled on. With the blood on the sides and above the door, the house/family would be completely protected.

In the very same way that the children of Israel applied the blood to their houses, we can apply Jesus' Blood today to enact that same protection. The Blood of *a* Lamb, *the* Lamb, *your* Lamb protects you because of covenant!

## PROTECTION FOR YOUR FAMILY

In an act similar to the Passover, Job continually offered blood sacrifices to protect his family. In fact, Job 1:5 tells us that Job's sacrifices had built a hedge of blood protection around his house and his family. But just two chapters later, Job says, *"For the thing which I greatly feared is come upon me, and that which I was afraid of is come unto me"* (Job 3:25). This tells us that Job had not been offering sacrifices out of faith, but from a place of fear. Regardless, God saw the blood and remained faithful to His covenant promises, and Job's family was protected.

*And it was so, when the days of their feasting were gone about, that Job sent and sanctified them, and rose up early in the morning, and offered burnt offerings according to the number of them all: for Job said, It may be that my sons have sinned, and cursed God in their hearts. Thus did Job continually* (Job 1:5).

When satan came against Job, it was no accident that he attacked the oxen and sheep first. He recognized the Lord's protection of Job and his family as a result of covenant blood.

*Hast not thou made an hedge about him, and about his house, and about all that he hath on every side? thou hast blessed the work of his hands, and his substance is increased in the land* (Job 1:10).

The enemy knew that when Job's livestock was destroyed, he would have no animal to offer in sacrifice. True to his nature, the enemy was there to interrupt the blood covenant and was very intentional about keeping Job from exercising his blood covenant rights.

*And there came a messenger unto Job, and said, The oxen were plowing, and the asses feeding beside them: and the Sabeans fell upon them, and took them away; yea, they have slain the servants with the edge of the sword; and I only am escaped alone to tell thee* (Job 1:14-15).

The enemy had no access to Job's family until he'd taken away his ability to offer blood sacrifices. When the animals were gone and there was no blood for Job to offer on behalf of his family, he was then susceptible to the enemy's attacks. The blood being applied for protection of their lives and family is why God told the Israelites the night of the Passover that none were to leave the house without first applying the blood of the lamb!

> *And ye shall take a bunch of hyssop, and dip it in the blood that is in the bason, and strike the lintel and the two side posts with the blood that is in the bason; and none of you shall go out at the door of his house until the morning* (Exodus 12:22).

They did not leave their homes before applying the lamb's blood, which is a powerful proclamation of their covenant. Likewise, we daily honor our covenant of the Lamb's protection over us and our families. Thank God, because of Jesus' sacrifice we are never without the covering of the once-and-for-all Blood sacrifice! Jesus' shed Blood is available to protect us and our families, but we must be careful to approach the Blood from a place of faith and not out of fear, as Job did. When our families are protected, our destinies are protected, as they are ultimately fulfilled in our future generations!

## WORTHY IS THE LAMB!

Our precious Lamb, Jesus, as the Lamb slain from the foundation of the world is the same Lamb we see standing in

Revelation 5. Just think, in the middle of everything going on in heaven there's a Lamb standing *"as though it had been slain"* (Rev. 5:6 NKJV)! This slain Lamb is *the* Lamb, our perfect Sacrifice—Jesus Himself.

> *And I beheld, and, lo, in the midst of the throne and of the four beasts, and in the midst of the elders, stood a Lamb as* [though] *it had been slain, having seven horns and seven eyes, which are the seven Spirits of God sent forth into all the earth* (Revelation 5:6).
>
> *And I beheld, and I heard the voice of many angels round about the throne and the beasts and the elders: and the number of them was ten thousand times ten thousand, and thousands of thousands; saying with a loud voice: Worthy is the Lamb that was slain to receive power, and riches, and wisdom, and strength, and honour, and glory, and blessing!* (Revelation 5:11-12).

The slain Lamb is the worthy Lamb. In heaven He is forever worshiped night and day. Verse 12 tells us that He is worthy to receive power, riches, wisdom, strength, honor, glory, and blessing. He's in heaven; why would He need to receive these things? I believe Jesus receives these things in heaven so He can give them to us, and this transaction actually took place at Calvary when He shed His Blood. It is part of our covenant rights, benefits, and privileges through our Blood covenant with Him! In fact, the seven things mentioned in Revelation 5:12 coordinate with Jesus'

Blood being shed from seven different places on His physical body. Let's look at them in order, as each of these places on His physical body correlates with an aspect of victory He won for us. They are our covenant rights through His shed Blood!

Worthy is the Lamb to receive:

### 1. Power

Jesus shed Blood from His feet when they pierced them with nails, giving us power over the enemy.

Power speaks of dominion over the devil. In Luke 10:19, Jesus told His disciples, *"Behold, I give unto you power to tread on serpents and scorpions, and over all the power of the enemy: and nothing shall by any means hurt you."* Treading on serpents and scorpions is something done with the feet. Jesus' feet were both pierced through at the same time. When the nails pierced Jesus' feet, He made power available to all who would call on His name. If you are a born-again believer, the enemy is also under your feet!

### 2. Riches

Jesus shed Blood from His left hand as they drove the nail through it into the cross, bringing provision to us in our covenant rights.

Proverbs 3:16 tells us that in wisdom's left hand are riches and honor. The left hand/side is always the side without favor. But here we see that wisdom's left hand is holding "riches and honor." This speaks of prosperity but also of knowing how to appropriate the blessing with honor when it comes. People sometimes live in lack because they are not wise or knowledgeable. When Jesus' left hand was pierced, He released the blessing that, no matter what, you can be brought into abundant provision and have wisdom to manage it well. When Jesus shed His Blood from His left hand, He was providing a way for you to not have to live in lack.

## 3. *Wisdom*

Jesus shed Blood from His head as they placed a crown of thorns upon his head, which gives us not only the mind of Christ but wisdom in our times of need.

> *The crown of the wise is their riches: but the foolishness of fools is folly* (Proverbs 14:24).

The crown of the wise speaks of the riches of the blessing that comes through Christ—it includes all the riches (monetary and otherwise) that come through having the mind of Christ and knowing how to appropriate these riches. When the crown of thorns pierced Jesus' head, the curse of poverty was broken and there came a release of wealth and wisdom available to all who would come to Him.

## 4. *Strength*

Jesus shed Blood from His back as they whipped Him 39 times with a whip having nine tails. This provided strength in every situation but also healing in our lives.

> *Who his own self bare our sins in his own body on the tree, that we, being dead to sins, should*

*live unto righteousness: by whose stripes ye were healed* (1 Peter 2:24).

*The plowers plowed upon my back: they made long their furrows* (Psalm 129:3).

The back speaks of strength and can also refer to divine healing. When Jesus shed Blood from His back, every kind of healing we need was made available to us. He bore our sins, our sicknesses, our griefs and sorrows. Through the stripes on Jesus' back, we were provided with both His strength and healing to appropriate whenever we need them.

### 5. Honor

Jesus shed Blood from His right hand as they pounded the nail into the wooden beam, which gave us the privilege of a long and honorable life in the blessings of our covenant.

Where the left hand contains riches and honor, the right hand holds the promise of a long and honorable life. "*Length of days is in her right hand*" (Prov. 3:16). Remember that the right hand is also the hand of blessing and favor, so the promise is that you'll find favor because you'll have the wisdom to live in the victory Jesus paid for. When Jesus' right hand was pierced, He purchased the promise of honor, favor, and long life for us. Under His Blood covenant, our destiny is to live a long life, full of honor and blessing.

### 6. Glory

Jesus shed Blood from His side as the soldiers pierced Him. The flowing blood and water signified the birthing of His church to live in the power and glory of His Kingdom benefits.

> *For a man indeed ought not to cover his head, forasmuch as he is the image and glory of God: but the woman is the glory of the man* (1 Corinthians 11:7).

When we see the word *glory* here, it's speaking of a reflection or an image. The side of Jesus' body represents glory. Just as Eve came from Adam's side and was a reflection of his "glory," the man is the glory of God. When Jesus' side was pierced, the glory of His Church was manifested. We also see the example of glory coming from the side of a person when Jesus spoke of the Holy Spirit's anointing coming from our bellies.

> *He that believeth on me, as the scripture hath said, out of his belly shall flow rivers of living water. (But this spake he of the Spirit, which they that believe on him should receive: for the Holy Ghost was not yet given; because that Jesus was not yet glorified)* (John 7:38-39).

Christ *in us* is our hope of glory. The well-known passage in Colossians points to this glory that's connected to our innermost being. This is the same glory that flowed when Jesus' side was pierced.

> *To whom God would make known what is the riches of the glory of this mystery among the Gentiles; which is Christ in you, the hope of glory* (Colossians 1:27).

### 7. Blessing

Jesus shed Blood from His forehead/face when His soul was vexed unto death, sweating great drops of blood that gave us not only eternal blessings but day-to-day blessings upon this earth and in this life.

*Blessings are upon the head of the just: but violence covereth the mouth of the wicked* (Proverbs 10:6).

In the Old Testament we see examples of fathers blessing their sons; a father would lay his hand on his sons' heads and speak life over them. The head is the place where blessings are given and received. The face is primarily how we identify and recognize one another. Our eyes, noses, and mouths are our main sources of expression and often reveal what's in our hearts. Being close to someone's face is an act of intimacy. Just as the psalmist in Psalm 27:8 said, *"When thou saidst, Seek ye my face; my heart said unto thee, Thy face, Lord, will I seek,"* our hearts cry out to see His face! As children of God, our greatest blessing is the blessing of His face. When Jesus' face was bloodied, He gave us full access to seek His face and find it!

Jesus' shed Blood is prophesied and visible to us throughout both the Old and New Testaments. His covenant is eternal, it's secure, and it's available to all who call upon His Name. This Blood was shed before the foundation of the world for you! This Lamb who was slain stands in the midst of all the glory of heaven. He holds all power, riches, wisdom, strength, honor, glory, and blessing, and

He is *your* Lamb! His precious shed Blood is the promise that these things are always available to you. In the middle of everything going on in your life, know that you are not alone—*the Lamb* is standing with you in the midst of every circumstance, and His shed Blood guarantees your victory!

## CHAPTER FIVE

# THE SPRINKLED BLOOD

As I mentioned at the start of this book, before I was ever saved, I had a relative who loved Jesus and taught me the significance of the protection of His Blood. I learned that by pleading the Blood over myself, the Lord would keep me safe. Throughout grade school and junior high, whenever I felt in danger, I would plead the Blood of Jesus as my protection. Although I had little understanding of what I was really doing, I knew the Blood of Jesus could and would protect me if I asked. When I would plead the Blood, I was applying its protecting and life-giving power over myself. It didn't work according to the level of my understanding; it worked because God is always faithful to His Blood covenant!

God wants us to live in the promises and protection of our covenant with Him. We must realize the benefits of Jesus' shed Blood, but we must also apply His Blood to our lives by "sprinkling." We've looked at how the *shed* Blood of Jesus contains all the rights and promises of the new covenant, so now let's look at how the *sprinkled* Blood activates the supernatural power of the covenant as we speak, claim, and confess its victory.

## APPLYING THE BLOOD

We already know the Passover points us to what is rightfully ours under the new covenant, but it can also help us to better understand the power and process of sprinkling the Blood of Jesus or what we often declare as pleading the Blood.

The account of the Passover in Exodus 12:22-23 is the first biblical reference to the sprinkling of blood:

> *And ye shall take a bunch of hyssop, and dip it in the blood that is in the bason, and strike the lintel and the two side posts with the blood that is in the bason; and none of you shall go out at the door of his house until the morning. For the Lord will pass through to smite the Egyptians; and when he seeth the blood upon the lintel, and on the two side posts, the Lord will pass over the door, and will not suffer the destroyer to come in unto your houses to smite you.*

A bunch of hyssop was to be taken and dipped in the blood, and then applied to the top and side posts of the

door. This applying of the blood was done through strik-
ing the lintel and the two side posts of the door. This act
of applying the blood was also referred to as sprinkling, as
mentioned in the book of Hebrews regarding the night of
the Passover.

> *Through faith* [Moses] *kept the passover, and the*
> *sprinkling of blood, lest he that destroyed the first-*
> *born should touch them* (Hebrews 11:28).

Every part of this process is significant and speaks to
us prophetically about how to sprinkle the Blood over our
own lives and why we can plead His Blood today!

First, hyssop was a type of plant with a watery substance in its roots, which would likely make it easy to
use for applying the blood to the doorposts. Its job here
was to take the blood from the basin and apply it. In the
same way, it is our privilege today and our responsibility to
plead and apply the Blood of Jesus over our lives, property,
and families.

Fast-forward to the New Testament—hyssop represents our tongues, or the words we speak. We see this
in Ephesians when Paul speaks to husbands about loving
their wives:

> *Husbands, love your wives, just as Christ also*
> *loved the church and gave Himself up for her, so*
> *that He might sanctify her, having cleansed her by*
> *the washing of water with the word* (Ephesians
> 5:25-26 NASB).

There is a connection here between water and words. This "washing of water" happened through what was spoken. It was a spiritual occurrence that was applied through something said.

The children of Israel applied the blood to their houses by sprinkling it with the hyssop. How do we "sprinkle" or apply the Blood of Jesus today? Just like with the water in Ephesians 5, we do it with our words!

Notice at the Passover that a "bunch" of hyssop was used to sprinkle the blood of the lamb (see Exod. 12:22). I believe this is not an accident or play on words but meant to show us that we can continually apply or plead the Blood a "bunch" of times! I like to make this my reminder that I need to apply the Blood of Jesus by speaking it a "bunch" of times every day—as often as I need!

The sprinkling might look something like this: "I am healed; I am saved; I am delivered; I am forgiven; I receive grace, mercy, and help in the time of need. Devil, you cannot touch my family, my finances, my destiny—I plead the Blood of Jesus!" These are more than just words—this is the *sprinkling* of the supernatural power contained in the Blood Jesus Christ shed for you! When you plead the Blood of Jesus, you are standing in a legal authority that the devil cannot contest. This sprinkling is a legal process, and when you stand under the Blood, you always win!

As long as the shed blood was left in the basin and not applied, the death angel had a right to strike that home. The blood had to be lifted out of the basin and sprinkled on the door to fulfill its purpose of protection; when the Lord saw the blood, He would not allow the destroyer access to that home.

This basin is a prophetic picture of the fountain mentioned in Zechariah 13:1—the *"fountain opened to the house of David and to the inhabitants of Jerusalem for sin and for uncleanness."* This basin and this fountain both speak of the fountain of Jesus' shed Blood that is always available to us! Like the children of Israel, we must take the bunch of hyssop (our mouths/our words), dip it into the basin (Jesus' shed Blood), and then apply the Blood to every area of our lives by speaking it. As we declare the Blood of Jesus, we are under God's supernatural protection that keeps the destroyer at a distance. It is the same thing as the Israelites sprinkling the blood using the hyssop!

The children of Israel were not allowed to leave their houses unless the blood had been applied, causing the enemy to pass them by. I encourage you to make this a regular practice—don't leave your house without pleading the Blood of Jesus over your home, your family, your pets, your belongings. Please understand that I'm not saying this out of legalism—this is a right and privilege of the new covenant that God wants us to enjoy! I'm also not saying we should do this out of any kind of fear of the enemy. We must be careful to speak from a place of faith, not from a place of fear as we know Job did when he offered blood sacrifices for his family. *"God has not given us a spirit of fear, but of power and of love and of a sound mind"* (2 Tim. 1:7 NKJV). It's so important that we're aware of the power of our words, especially the power of the Blood that is activated as we sprinkle it on a regular basis.

When Jesus sat with His disciples at the Last Supper (Passover), He told them, *"I will not drink of the fruit of the vine, until the kingdom of God shall come"* (Luke 22:18). The "fruit of the vine" was vinegar or sour wine. In Matthew 27, as He was being crucified, He was offered *"vinegar to drink mingled with gall: and when he had tasted thereof, he would not drink"* (Matt. 27:34). Did you see that? Jesus wouldn't drink the vinegar (sour wine / fruit of the vine) at this point because it wasn't yet time for Him to do so. But let's look at where and when Jesus *did* drink of the fruit of the vine.

> *After this, Jesus knowing that all things were now accomplished, that the scripture might be fulfilled, saith, I thirst. Now there was set a vessel full of vinegar: and they filled a spunge with vinegar, and put it upon hyssop, and put it to his mouth. When Jesus therefore had received the vinegar, he said, It is finished: and he bowed his head, and gave up the ghost* (John 19:28-30).

Remember that He'd told the disciples that He wouldn't drink *"until the kingdom of God shall come"* (Luke 22:18). At this point, He was just moments away from death when He said, *"I thirst."* I believe He was not only thirsting for natural drink, but He was also thirsting for the Kingdom of God to come to earth. Notice *how* He is given a drink: "they filled a sponge with vinegar, and *put it on hyssop*, and put it to his mouth" (see John 19:29). It was only when the hyssop had touched Jesus' mouth that the Kingdom He'd been thirsting for came.

Once again there is a key connection between hyssop and the mouth, or our words. On the cross, Jesus' words, *"It is finished,"* declared that His Kingdom had come. When we speak words of life, we actually cause the power and blessing of the Kingdom to manifest in our lives and in the earth!

Revelation 12:11 tells us the ones who overcame the enemy did so through the Blood of Lamb and *"the word of their testimony"* and by loving Jesus more than their own lives. Our words are a key part of how we overcome the enemy! Whatever we speak and declare with our mouths is what will manifest in our lives.

> *Death and life are in the power of the tongue: and they that love it shall eat the fruit thereof* (Proverbs 18:21).

This verse is reminding us to choose life over death and speak words of faith rather than negative words that produce negative results. We must declare life! Apply *life* over yourself and your family! We do this by speaking right, applying the Blood rights of our covenant, and declaring the promises of His Word. We need to do this both over the doorposts of our lives but also our homes like Israel was instructed on the night of the Passover.

## THE MEZUZAH

One way the Israelites remembered the powerful protection and deliverance God gave them that Passover evening when they applied the blood was through a scroll placed at their doorposts. This is referred to as the mezuzah. It's a kosher parchment scroll that is rolled up and put into a decorative case and placed on the doorposts of the home in observance of Deuteronomy 11:20: *"And thou shalt write them upon the door posts of thine house, and upon thy gates"* (also see Deut. 6:4-9 and 11:13-21).

The children of Israel put the mezuzot (plural) on the doorposts of their homes during their liberation from the bondage of Egypt. To this day, traditional Jewish families place mezuzot at the entrances to their homes. Throughout history, these mezuzot have served as daily reminders that the children of Israel were bought with a price and that their homes are dedicated to God.

God was essentially saying, "When I see the blood on the door, I will stand in front of your door, in front of your money, in front of your children, in front of your marriage, and I will forbid the angel of death to destroy your family!" The same protection is available for believers in Jesus Christ as we apply the Word of God and plead the Blood of Jesus.

At the Passover, the blood on the doorpost was a type of the Old Testament mezuzah. The New Testament equivalent would be the act of applying the Word and pleading the Blood of Jesus over our homes, protecting our families and possessions.

We can also look at this from the perspective of our bodies/ourselves being the "house" that is protected by the

Blood. When we've been oppressed by the enemy and he leaves as a result of healing or deliverance, Scripture is clear about his activity. In Matthew 12:43-45, Jesus tells us that:

> *When an unclean spirit goes out of a man, it passes through dry places seeking rest, but finds none. Then it says, "I will return to my house from which I came." And when it comes, it finds it empty, swept, and put in order. Then it goes and brings with itself seven other spirits more evil than itself, and they enter and dwell there. And the last state of that man is worse than the first. So shall it be also with this evil generation* (MEV).

How does the unclean spirit know that the house is swept and clean and garnished? I believe it's because the door is still open. It can see into the house, and it realizes these people have not put Jesus' shed Blood on their home and lives. (Remember when we elaborated on the seven places from which Jesus shed His Blood the last chapter?)

That mezuzah on the doorpost is a reminder that every curse is broken by the seven places Jesus shed His Blood, and every blessing they represent has been released. In the same way, we place a spiritual "mezuzah" between ourselves and the enemy when we speak and apply the Blood today. Moses tells the people in Deuteronomy 28:7:

> *The Lord will cause your enemies who rise against you to be defeated before your face; they shall*

*come out against you one way and flee before you seven ways* (NKJV).

When we stand in the fullness of our covenant promises, we can tell the enemy, "Devil, you may have come in one way, but you're fleeing seven different ways by the Blood of the Lamb!"

The mezuzah is a reminder to you and a sign to the enemy that not only your house but also your body is Blood-bought; you are Blood-covered; you have the anointing of God! God Himself will stand not only at the door of your house but also your life and make every angel of darkness pass you by. It is your covenant right and proclamation that the enemy isn't coming into your house anymore, and he's not bringing any demons back either!

## SPRINKLING THE BLOOD ON THE WORD AND THE PEOPLE

The greatest blessing of our Blood covenant is the access God has given us to His presence. It is His greatest desire to fellowship with us, His children—and everything else contained in our covenant is there to bring us into the joy of experiencing His presence and to enjoy a blessed life in Him! Exodus 24 points to this fellowship as we see the blood sprinkled on the word and on the people.

In Exodus 24:1-11, God made a covenant agreement with Israel. He had promised them before that if they would obey His words, *"I will take you as My people, and I will be your God"* (Exod. 6:7). Moses then sprinkled the blood on the book of the law/Word *and* the people (see Exod. 24:8). After Moses read the law to the people, they answered, "We understand, and we will obey" (see Exod. 24:7).

By answering the law/Word Moses read with their declaration, the people were expressing that they believed God's promises and they were receiving them. Through their spoken words, they were agreeing with the covenant of the Lord.

It wasn't just that a lamb had been sacrificed or slain, but the lamb's blood had to also be applied or sprinkled as we see when Moses applied it to the book of the law and upon the people. This act of sprinkling the lamb's blood is what sealed or ratified the covenant; it would make it valid. Hebrews tells us that Moses *"took the blood…and sprinkled both the book, and all the people"* (Heb. 9:19). God wanted the blood applied to the people *and* sprinkled on the book.

The principle and process apply to us today—the Lamb has been slain, but the Lord wants us to plead (sprinkle) the Blood. Our words are the "hyssop" that apply Jesus' shed Blood to our lives. "Sprinkling the book," for us, means that we declare the Word of God. Jesus Himself was the "Word made flesh," and declaring Scripture is another way that we verbalize our covenant promises. It's so important that we remind ourselves daily, and as often as needed, of our covenant. It's not just the enemy and the powers of darkness who need to hear our declarations—we need to hear ourselves speak our covenant promises. As we hear our own words, it builds our faith. *"So then faith cometh by hearing, and hearing by the Word of God"* (Rom. 10:17).

> *Let the redeemed of the Lord say so, whom he hath redeemed from the hand of the enemy* (Psalm 107:2).

Consider this: how are we redeemed? By the Blood, right? Jesus' Blood has made us *"the redeemed."* And this psalm tells us we are to *"say so!"* This is how we "sprinkle" the Blood.

Sprinkling the Blood is not just speaking our covenant benefits and promises while we spend little time in fellowship with Him. We must never forget that His precious Blood gave us access to come into His presence and enjoy a life of intimacy and communion with Him. In Exodus 24:9-11, Moses, Nadab, Abihu, and the seventy elders went up to the mountain to meet God after they had been sprinkled with the blood of a lamb. They were able to be in the presence of God as the Lord appeared to them, coming down a sapphire-stone walk. These men saw a table spread before them, and they sat in God's presence and ate and drank with Him:

> *And upon the nobles of the children of Israel he laid not his hand: also they saw God, and did eat and drink* (Exodus 24:11).

On this occasion, it wasn't only about the forgiveness/ remission of sin; this was about how sprinkling/applying the blood gave them communion with God. As the blood had been applied, they were now sanctified, cleansed, and fit to be in God's presence! Think about this: He prepares a table before you in the presence of your enemies—those who cannot touch you because of the Blood of Jesus! (See Psalm 23.)

If these men had access to see God and to eat and drink with Him, how much more do you have access through the Blood of *the* Lamb, *your* Lamb, Jesus? When we apply the Blood by speaking it and by declaring God's Word, His presence is increased in our lives!

The ultimate purpose of Jesus shedding His precious Blood was to bring us back into perfect, joyful fellowship with the Father. It is only His shed Blood that gives us the assurance of the relationship we were created for.

> *Having therefore, brethren, boldness to enter into the holiest by the blood of Jesus, by a new and living way, which he hath consecrated for us, through the veil, that is to say, his flesh; and having an high priest over the house of God; let us draw near with a true heart in full assurance of faith, having our hearts sprinkled from an evil conscience, and our bodies washed with pure water* (Hebrews 10:19-22).

The Blood of Jesus is life-giving; it's powerful; it makes us overcomers. It speaks a better word over us than any accusation or curse of the enemy. His Blood has forever settled our case in heaven, and it's legally rendered us righteous, redeemed, and free. We can now live victorious, fulfilled lives because we have been redeemed by the Blood of the perfect, spotless Lamb!

When we take time to search the Scriptures, we discover so many life-giving and life-changing treasures the Lord has provided us through His Blood covenant. The key is, we must look for them (see Prov. 25:2). God doesn't want us to merely have head knowledge of the covenant He made with His own Blood; He wants us to search out His treasures and walk in the blessing and authority He died to give us. Jesus' sacrifice has broken every curse over our lives and has sealed our victory. I encourage you to make it your daily privilege to plead/sprinkle the supernatural power of His Blood. When you do you will live such an amazing, healthy, blessed, protected, and prospered life!

## SOME TRUTHS OF SCRIPTURE YOU CAN DECLARE

- The Blood of Jesus is the Blood of the new covenant, which has been shed for me (see Luke 22:20).

- The Blood of Jesus is the Blood of the everlasting covenant, which is in force for me for all eternity (see Heb. 13:20).

- The life is in the Blood of Jesus; therefore, the very life of God lives in my spirit and flows into my soul (mind, will, and emotions) and into my physical body (see Gen. 9:4; Lev. 17:11).

- Through faith in the Blood of Jesus I have been redeemed—bought from the hand of the enemy. Therefore, I am no longer in the kingdom of darkness, but through the Blood I have been translated into the Kingdom of God's dear Son (see Col. 1:13-14; Eph. 1:7; 1 Pet. 1:18-19; Acts 20:28; Heb. 9:12).

- The Blood of Jesus is very precious to me because of its cleansing power from all sin and unrighteousness, which includes all the consequences and effects of sin (see 1 John 1:7,9; Heb. 10:10-25; Rev. 19:7-9).

- Through the precious Blood of Jesus, I have been made unto God a king and a priest, and have been given authority to reign with Him on the earth now and for all eternity (see Rev. 5:9-10; Rom. 5:17 AMP).

# PART 2

# BLOOD, WATER, SPIRIT: OUR PATTERN FOR ABUNDANT LIFE

# CHAPTER SIX

# THESE THREE AGREE: THE BLOOD, WATER, AND SPIRIT

Throughout this book, we have looked at the power of the Blood and the many wonderful benefits of our covenant with God. We have discovered that the supernatural Blood of Jesus is the very foundation of our lives as believers, but if we look closely, we see that God reveals another amazing truth to us. It is in the pattern of the Blood, water, and Spirit, (we will look at it in this order) that is woven throughout Scripture. This pattern isn't just a good idea from God—I believe it's a way that He reveals His intention for us to walk in fullness as believers. We'll examine this pattern, and you may be surprised at how many times it shows up through both the Old and New Testaments, but more importantly we'll learn to appropriate it in our lives!

The Word tells us that just as there are three in heaven—Father, Son, and Holy Spirit—and there are three that bear witness on earth that together form the perfect testimony of Jesus. In addition, it is also a prophetic prototype meant for every believer that we need to add our agreement.

> *This is he that came by water and blood, even Jesus Christ; not by water only, but by water and blood. And it is the Spirit that beareth witness, because the Spirit is truth. For there are three that bear record in heaven, the Father, the Word, and the Holy Ghost: and these three are one. And there are three that bear witness in earth, the Spirit, and the water, and the blood: and these three agree in one* (1 John 5:6-8).

The Scripture reveals that it is the Spirit and the water and the Blood that agree here on the earth. Notice in this verse the order in which this pattern is mentioned. It is the Spirit, the water, and the Blood. However, we will refer to this pattern in the order of the Blood, water, and Spirit through the remaining chapters. Our life in Christ starts with the Blood at our salvation through the cross, followed by our dedication to this decision by baptism in water, to a daily life filled with Holy Spirit. Yet if you look at this verse mentioned in 1 John, the pattern is Spirit, water, and then the Blood. The Spirit mentioned first is our powerful new life in Christ, baptized in the Holy Spirit, followed by the foundations of a converted life (water) and a true born-again experience by the Blood.

In the following pages, we will look at these elements of the Spirit, water, and the Blood, as well as the significance of this pattern for us, as each has their own unique prophetic application. God communicates this prophetic pattern all throughout the Bible, but it is most clear in Jesus' baptism/ministry, crucifixion, and the coming of the Holy Spirit on the Day of Pentecost.

These three elements are represented this way in the life of Jesus:

- Water: Jesus' baptism/ministry
- Blood: Jesus' crucifixion
- Spirit: the coming of the Holy Spirit

## The Crucifixion, Resurrection, and the Ascension

This pattern of the Blood, water, and Spirit is also reflected in the crucifixion, the resurrection, and the ascension of Jesus Christ. For example, the Blood represents the crucifixion as it was a bloody sacrifice as Jesus shed His Blood. The water is a type of not only His baptism but also of His resurrection. How is this, you might ask? In baptism, one is submerged in water and raised up from the water, symbolizing our new life in Christ. It also prophetically speaks of how Jesus was placed in a tomb and emerged from the grave in His resurrection, giving us all a newness of life and eternal life. Last, the ascension is likened to the Spirit because once Jesus ascended and was seated at His Father's right hand the Holy Spirit was then released.

It's one thing to understand these powerful prototypes as they pertain to Jesus and what He fulfilled for us. So what does this mean for us personally? As we discovered, the Blood represents the cross and the bloody sacrifice that He gave for us. It is to remind us that we can only be saved when we come to the cross and receive forgiveness of sins through His Blood. The water, likened to His resurrection, is to be a reminder of being truly converted to a new life in Christ accompanied by a holy lifestyle. As in baptism, we are fully immersed into the water to symbolize our old sinful nature is to be under submission, immersed, and resurrected in a new converted spiritual walk and life. Now the Spirit mentioned in John's epistle reveals to us how we too, like the 120 in the upper room after the Lord's ascension, need to receive this promise and be endued with power on high as they were (see Acts 1:8)!

This prophetic pattern is showing us as believers how to live the fullest life possible in Christ. In order to do this, our lives must be patterned in this same way. In other words:

- Blood: After we receive salvation, we must also continually apply the Blood of Jesus and appropriate its benefits day to day.
- Water: We need to have a true conversion and acknowledge Jesus as our Lord and Savior.

- Spirit: We are to receive the baptism of the Holy Spirit, not as just a one-time experience, but to be continually filled with the Spirit and walk in His power.

It is important that we always pay attention when Scripture shows us a pattern. In the same way, we must give attention to the pattern of Blood, water, and Spirit, because they testify of what belongs to us as believers in Jesus Christ and are mentioned so much throughout the Bible.

Remember, when the Lord gave Moses instructions for building the tabernacle, He said, *"see to it that you make them according to the pattern which was shown you on the mountain"* (Exod. 25:40 NKJV).

> *Who serve unto the example and shadow of heavenly things, as Moses was admonished of God when he was about to make the tabernacle: for, See, saith he, that thou make all things according to the pattern shewed to thee in the mount* (Hebrews 8:5).

How does this "building" or "tabernacle," which was prophetically foreshadowed in what Moses built, relate to us today? Just like the Old Testament tabernacle where God's presence lived, we too are to be carriers of His presence. We must know what brings and maintains His presence in our lives. This means, as members of the Body of Christ, we are now the "tabernacles" or the places God has chosen to dwell. Just like Moses was instructed, I believe part of this building that causes the Lord to dwell in our lives in a greater level is when we "build" ourselves up in the revelation of His Word. This is especially true in the understanding of the Blood, water, and Spirit. When we have a strong foundation of understanding our Blood covenant and knowing how to appropriate its benefits, we then live a deeper converted life as a believer, which attracts the Spirit of God to us in a stronger, more tangible way.

## WATER, BLOOD, AND SPIRIT CHRISTIANS

Therefore, we must not just settle for praying a salvation prayer but live fully converted, with a life endued with the Spirit of God. When looking at the pattern of Blood, water, and Spirit, I see a parallel to the way believers often live their lives. I call them "Blood Christians," "water Christians," and "Spirit Christians." Let me explain.

Blood Christians are those who understand salvation is not by works, but they go to the other extreme. They profess that the Blood of Jesus has forgiven them of everything, and therefore they can live however they want. They may not say this is their intent, but their lifestyle is one that reflects this attitude. These are often proponents of the hyper-grace message, which is often an excuse for sinful, reckless living. Sadly, they've misconstrued the concept of being cleansed by the Blood as permission to live lives that don't honor God, or anyone else, but mainly seek to serve themselves because they are under grace. This mindset is what has caused preachers and congregations to become carnal and accepting of the culture that is filled with compromise, all because they are trying to reach the unsaved. We are instructed in Scripture to be in the world but not of it. In other words, we don't need to cheapen the Blood or His grace by compromise, sin, or "relevance" to the culture to reach them! Jesus never compromised Himself or His message in order to evangelize the lost. He also held His disciples and followers to a high level of repentance and living according to the kingdom of God. This means as true Christians, we must *not* cheapen the Blood through halfhearted, carnal, and compromised Christianity because we are saved by the Blood!

Now, let's look at water Christians. These water Christians are those who may have been baptized at birth and who believe their church affiliation, their parents' religious practices, or their denominational label is their way unto salvation. They are living from their water experience—their infant baptism or their good works—rather than coming to Jesus for salvation followed by a mature, converted life in Christ. They may not actually even be saved but going through religious traditions.

Another example of a water Christian is one who understands salvation by the blood of Jesus, but now that they are saved they live in a form of religious legalism. This doesn't mean "anything goes Christianity," but often these people think they are living in spiritual freedom when in reality it is man-made tradition. They often choose Bible verses to show their religious holiness, while the issue is often man's preference and not something defined as evil by Scripture or the Lord Himself.

The danger of water Christians today is, while they will acknowledge they need to be saved by the Blood and even baptized in water, it stops there. They are saved because they "prayed a prayer" followed by being baptized. They never go deeper to live in the knowledge of their Blood covenant, followed by a life that is deeply committed daily to spiritual character and fruit. For some it might be that they haven't been taught that there is more available in their covenant with God. Yet sadly, some are just satisfied with their salvation experience and baptism and don't press in for more. This can be seen in modern Christianity that often defends the world's standards over kingdom mandates and standards. If that is not enough, these relevant water Christians will even reject or ignore a life pressing in for more of the Spirit of God and for His standard of righteous living.

A true Christian is one who is truly converted, changed, and living a repentant life. It's not just praying a prayer of salvation to be saved but a continued, daily choice to live godly as a true convert of Christ. We need the combination of Blood, water, and Spirit in our lives. We need to get saved through Jesus' Blood. Then, the Scripture commands that we be water baptized. This does not refer to infant baptism, but rather is an outward declaration and profession of faith by someone who has been saved and reborn through the Blood of Jesus. The process of going under the water is a burying and washing away of the old life, and the rising up out of the water signifies the person is now a new creation in Christ. Again, this is not salvation, but is the outward expression of the change that occurs when we are born again.

Finally, the last element that we identify with as believers in this prophetic pattern is Spirit. When we are Spirit Christians, we come into agreement with what God approved. God approved of the Blood, He approved of the water, and when He sent His Holy Spirit at Pentecost, He was inviting us to come into agreement with Him that Jesus' sacrifice was accepted and approved because of His shed Blood! No more sacrifices would be needed. Spirit Christians are those who have been saved and really understand their Blood covenant, water baptized and converted, followed by being baptized in the Holy Spirit with the evidence of speaking in tongues. These Spirit Christians are full of power!

According to the prophetic pattern of the Blood, water, and Spirit, a Spirit Christian is one who not only understands salvation by grace but also how vital daily choices are and how we must live a holy lifestyle. A Spirit Christian doesn't just settle for eternal life only but also appropriates and understands their Blood covenant rights because they know Jesus paid for more than just forgiveness of sins. A Spirit Christian will never settle for worldliness or be dictated by cultural redefining of standards, truths, or definitions. They stand strong in their convictions, holding and carrying the bloodstained banner of Christ high in their hearts. Their life is truly reflected as a radical believer who causes all hell to fear their revelation, standards, and appropriation of the Blood of Christ!

## THREE TYPES OF CHURCHES: BLOOD, WATER, AND SPIRIT

There are not just Blood, water, and Spirit Christians but also the same pattern is seen with churches. This is important to discern and understand. In Christendom today, churches or preachers get stuck in just one revelation. When they do, they never walk in the full revelation, benefit, or power that all three bring.

So just what prophetically are Blood, water, and Spirit churches? Let's start with what I will refer to as a Blood church. We know that the Blood speaks of the cross. There are some churches today that choose only to preach about the cross and seldom move deeper in the power of His resurrection. Their services either reject or ignore the supernatural power of God available by the Holy Spirit. The cross is preached to bring people to repentance and salvation.

Now, we fully understand that we must preach the cross, as it is the foundation and is extremely important to our Christian faith. However, it is not just preaching about the cross only; we must add the revelation of the water (conversion) and the Spirit (signs, wonders, miracles, and the Holy Spirit's baptism and power). This is why it mentions in 1 John 5 all three are in agreement and not just one.

In addition, in Blood churches, the pastor can be more about trends than true conversion, as in a water church, or Holy Spirit power as in Spirit churches. This is why you may never see the power of God demonstrated and the

Holy Spirit moving in their services because it is only about making the visitor comfortable and appealing to the lost.

Blood and water churches both preach the power of the cross. Yet we also need the preaching of a lifestyle change, which is a water church. In addition to the cross, these churches bring people to maturity through conversion—or water. However, this is not to be the exclusive message or expression. We need churches that preach the cross (Blood), true conversion (water), and then move on to a powerful life in the Spirit's power like on the day of Pentecost (Spirit). The demonstration of the Holy Spirit marks a Spirit church.

Sadly, there are some churches that are not any of these three—Blood, water, or Spirit. Some churches take the message of the Blood and water it down or ignore it. Seldom if ever are the people attending taught the way of salvation or instructed to repent of sin and accept Jesus, not just as Savior but Lord. Then there are water churches that may preach the cross but don't progress to bring their congregations to a place of Christian maturity. They may baptize their members in water as a religious practice and ordinance but do little to hold them to a standard of righteousness based on God's Word and Kingdom rather than the current culture and trends.

A Blood or water church that is only focused on the cross exclusively can be in danger of becoming seeker-sensitive, user-friendly, and void of any supernatural power of the Holy Spirit. This is due to their belief that all church services are for the purpose of winning the lost, even if they must shackle the Holy Spirit, so to speak. Rather than the Holy Spirit and His power being the welcomed guest in their services, they put more focus on the visitor. We must not forget that on the day of Pentecost Peter boldly preached the cross, dealing with the need for the listeners to be saved through the Blood. He then went on to preach the importance of being baptized in water, repenting, and truly being converted, followed by receiving the gift of the Holy Ghost.

> *Then Peter said unto them, Repent, and be baptized every one of you in the name of Jesus Christ for the remission of sins, and ye shall receive the gift of the Holy Ghost* (Acts 2:38).

Peter welcomed the Holy Spirit and instructed them to receive the Holy Spirit and be prepared to speak in a new heavenly language. Neither Peter nor the Holy Spirit were intimidated by those visiting that day in Jerusalem, and the Bible records that there were many.

> *And there were dwelling at Jerusalem Jews, devout men, out of every nation under heaven* (Acts 2:5).

This is why churches should not exclude or limit the Holy Spirit based on who is attending. Neither should we tailor all our services to be exclusively evangelistic in presentation and focus. Altar calls are vital for those in the church and should also be offered to minister to the lost, but they should not replace an important reason one is called to pastor. Primarily, it is to also bring the church to maturity while equipping them to do the work of the ministry (see Eph. 4). This includes going outside the four walls of the church and evangelizing the lost, so they can come to our churches, grow, change, and be filled with the Holy Spirit and see His power demonstrated in our services!

It is important that we have all three expressions and revelations in the prophetic pattern and not just be a Spirit church either. What do I mean by this? Yes, we should hunger for the Holy Spirit and the demonstration of His power, but we also need to ground our people in a strong foundation of the Blood (cross) and Christian discipleship and maturity (water).

When churches don't have all three manifestations of the Blood, water, and Spirit in the prophetic pattern, they become out of focus and balance. This is especially true when the Holy Spirit is pushed out and quenched, as well as when the church is kept in a spiritual state of immaturity through watered-down messages or messages that only appeal to the lost. We must reach the lost, but not at the expense of people being taught, discipled, and encouraged to be truly converted to Jesus Christ. This comes by bold preaching and not being immersed in this culture or taking on a belief system and lifestyle of worldliness, as some churches, preachers, and Christians have done, sadly.

Then some churches progress beyond salvation-oriented services and focus on encouraging salvation and conversion, but they do it more by works than by the power of the Holy Spirit. In this kind of church or setting you will not hear people speaking in tongues on Sunday or see many Holy Spirit expressions or manifestations. This again is not according to the prophetic pattern God has shown us in the Blood, water, and Spirit. They may be preaching the cross and baptism in water to be converted, but they are excluding the third part of what we are to agree with—the Holy Spirit. Some even go on to say, "We don't need to be filled with the Holy Spirit and speak in tongues. Miracles, signs, and wonders have passed away." Yet we must understand that, just as the Father, Son, and the Holy Spirit are in agreement in heaven, the Blood, water, and Spirit must be in agreement in the earth, in our lives, and in our churches as well.

In the remaining chapters, we are going to look at some of the many instances where this pattern is repeated throughout the Bible. My prayer is that no matter how you've been living up until now, you'll understand and run after the Holy Spirit by the time we're through.

# CHAPTER SEVEN

# THE PROPHETIC PATTERN OF THE BLOOD, WATER, AND SPIRIT

Let's start at the beginning in Genesis to discover the prophetic pattern of the Blood, water, and Spirit. We first see this pattern in creation when the *Spirit* moved upon the *waters* and the *blood* began to flow when God breathed His life into Adam. Remember that Leviticus 17:11 tells us that *"the life of the flesh is in the blood."* God's breath started the flow of blood throughout Adam's body. Again, God was establishing a pattern that would reveal His full plan for us as believers. From the very time of the Spirit moving across the waters to the blood flowing in Adam's body, we see this pattern. I don't believe it is a coincidence that the order in creation was the Spirit, water, and the Blood as we mentioned in the previous chapter. This is exactly the order we see that the apostle John mentioned agrees in the earth!

> *And these three are one. And there are three that bear witness in earth, the Spirit, and the water, and the blood: and these three agree in one* (1 John 5:7b-8).

This shows us how important these three are to the Lord and how much we need to add our agreement to this divine order and plan for our lives. Let's look more closely at this pattern as God was creating the heavens, the earth, and man.

## In the Beginning

> *And the Spirit of God moved upon the face of the waters* (Genesis 1:2b).

The Spirit of God was moving upon the face of the water! Not only was God's Spirit moving across the deep, but it was also in a time of darkness.

> *And the earth was without form, and void; and darkness was upon the face of the deep. And the Spirit of God moved upon the face of the waters* (Genesis 1:2).

This is important to know, as God always shows up and moves when it is dark in the earth or our lives. The state of the earth—without form, void, and dark—also prophetically reveals to us that God has a plan of redemption. What is that plan? The plan would be the divine pattern of the Blood, water, and Spirit! Remember, it would involve the Blood of Jesus and the cross, the water of His baptism and resurrection, and His ascension with the sending of the Holy Spirit. Not only was the Lord establishing creation's order, but He was bringing forth this prophetic pattern, starting with the Spirit moving upon the water, followed by the creation of a man in His image. It wouldn't be just a man made from the earth's soil, but a man who would carry the very life and Blood of his Creator.

> *And the Lord God formed man of the dust of the ground, and breathed into his nostrils the breath of life; and man became a living soul* (Genesis 2:7).

When the Lord created man, He made him from the dust of the ground and then breathed into this lifeless body. Imagine what happened next. This man's heart began to beat for the first time, and his eyes opened as his chest breathed out the very breath and life of God Himself! What caused all this life to begin in this man? It was blood that flowed through his veins because of God's breath giving him life.

This was no ordinary man; it was a man created in God's image with blood that came from God. This is why the man the Lord created would be called *Adam*. Why Adam? It was to signify this life and blood that was given by God. You see, the name *Adam* means "blood man." The word relates to the two Hebrew words—*dam*, "blood," and *adamah*, "earth/ground." These words show us that the basic meaning of Adam was associated with both "blood" and "ground." Adam and creation would reveal on the earth this heavenly pattern of the Blood, water, and Spirit. It would not only be redemption's plan, but also what man would walk in to bring them into the blessing of the covenant.

## LEVITICUS AND THE BLOOD, WATER, AND SPIRIT

Next, in the book of Leviticus this same pattern points to redemption's plan fulfilled in Jesus' crucifixion and resurrection:

> *And the priest shall go forth out of the camp; and the priest shall look, and, behold, if the plague of leprosy be healed in the leper; then shall the priest command to take for him that is to be cleansed two birds alive and clean, and cedar wood, and scarlet, and hyssop: and the priest shall command that one of the birds be killed in an earthen vessel over running water: as for the living bird, he shall take it, and the cedar wood, and the scarlet, and the hyssop, and shall dip them and the living bird in the blood of the bird that was killed over the running water: and he shall sprinkle upon him that is to be cleansed from the leprosy seven times, and shall pronounce him clean, and shall let the living bird loose into the open field. And he that is to be cleansed shall wash his clothes* (Leviticus 14:3-8a).

Here, leprosy represents our condition apart from the Lord—we need to be cleansed from our sins as the leper needed to be cleansed from his disease through water. The next thing for the leper was for blood to be shed by a lamb sacrifice, as we see in the continuation of Leviticus 14. Yet it is important to first mention the prophetic act of shedding the blood of birds, pointing again to God's redemptive plan. One of the two birds would be killed, while the other bird would be set free. What does this mean? The living bird that was released foreshadowed Jesus' crucifixion followed by His resurrection. In addition, we see cedar wood, scarlet, and hyssop pointing us to Jesus. Cedar wood represents the cross, scarlet represents Jesus' Blood, and, as we know, hyssop symbolizes the applying of the Blood.

The first bird represents Jesus' crucifixion; it is to be killed in an earthen vessel, symbolic of Jesus' body. The running water refers to the water that flowed from His side when it was pierced on the cross.

The second, living bird represents the resurrected Jesus, and again, cedar wood represents the cross. This living bird was dipped into the blood of the bird that was killed, and it was then released into the open field, symbolic of resurrection. But notice that this only occurs after the leper is sprinkled with the blood and pronounced clean. The entire picture is that we are only cleansed and whole by the Blood of Jesus, who was first crucified and then resurrected!

Farther along in this same chapter, we find the Spirit, water, and Blood pattern. It is important to remember that oil is symbolic of the Holy Spirit. The leper who was washed with the water of cleansing would now be required to have the blood of a lamb applied to him in three specific places. Pay close attention to the places the blood would be applied on this leper as well as the oil. Not only does it further establish the prophetic pattern of the Blood, water, and Spirit but it points to the places Jesus shed His blood as part of God's plan of redeeming man!

> *And the priest shall wave them for a wave offering before the Lord: and he shall kill the lamb of the trespass offering, and the priest shall take some of the blood of the trespass offering, and put it upon the tip of the right ear of him that is to be cleansed, and upon the thumb of his right hand, and upon the great toe of his right foot: and the priest shall pour of the oil into the palm of his own left hand: and the priest shall sprinkle with his right finger some of the oil that is in his left hand seven times before the Lord: and the priest shall put of the oil that is in his hand upon the tip of the right ear of him that is to be cleansed, and upon the thumb of his right hand, and upon the great toe of his right foot, upon the place of the blood of the trespass offering: and the rest of the oil that is in the priest's hand he shall put upon the head of him that is to be cleansed, to make an atonement for him before the Lord* (Leviticus 14:24-29).

These verses point us to what happened at the cross, as they specifically tell of the Blood that was on the head, hands, and feet of Jesus. Blood was also applied to the leper's head, hands, and feet, followed by the oil in the same way. What does this point to for our lives as believers? This reveals prophetically the power of our Blood covenant. The Blood is applied to the head for our minds. The hands represent putting our covenant to remembrance or appropriating our covenant rights of blessing. Last, the Blood applied to the feet is not only the authority we have through our Blood covenant but also means we should walk continually in our Blood covenant rights, privileges, and benefits.

We see the oil applied to the very same places—the head, hands, and feet. This is because when Jesus shed His Blood, the Holy Spirit was released and is now given to us as believers to walk in the powerful anointing of the Holy Spirit. We now have pure, powerful wisdom, knowledge, and the mind of Christ because of the Holy Spirit, as represented in the oil upon the head of the leper. We also have the powerful anointing in our hands to lay them upon the sick so they recover and to display the mighty acts of the Lord in and through us. If that is not enough, we can walk in the Spirit with our feet and not fulfill the lusts of the flesh but walk in the power of the Holy Spirit. Thank God for His plan of redemption but also His prophetic pattern of the Blood, water, and Spirit beautifully foreshadowed with the leper.

Prophetically, these verses speak of the life of salvation we have through Jesus' shed Blood, followed by baptism in water, which is a witness of our new life in Christ. This is followed by the oil that is sprinkled and applied by the priest to the one needing to be cleansed. This represents the anointing and baptism of the Holy Spirit, our evidence of a power-filled life!

Again, we see this prophetic pattern as it starts with the water. Remember that the leper had to be washed in water. Then, we see the blood from a lamb applied to the same places Jesus was wounded during His crucifixion—head, hands, and feet. Finally, we see the Spirit represented by the application of the oil to the same places as the blood—head, hands, and feet. All to reveal redemption and God's prophetic pattern!

Never forget, 1 John 5 says that *"there are three that bear witness on earth: the Spirit, the water, and the blood; and these three agree as one"* (1 John 5:8 NKJV).

## POLLUTED IN BLOOD, WASHED IN WATER, AND ANOINTED WITH OIL

I want to continue to show you this powerful plan of redemption and prophetic pattern as revealed in the book of Ezekiel. We find this pattern in Ezekiel 16 when he describes the relationship between God and Israel. It is also a picture of everyone born into this world. He begins to prophesy revealing their sinful condition and the sinful condition of mankind, so much that even their blood was polluted.

*None eye pitied thee, to do any of these unto thee,*
*to have compassion upon thee; but thou wast cast*

*out in the open field, to the lothing of thy person, in the day that thou wast born. And when I passed by thee, and saw thee polluted in thine own blood, I said unto thee when thou wast in thy blood, Live; yea, I said unto thee when thou wast in thy blood, Live* (Ezekiel 16:5-6).

We also see in these verses a picture of the fallen, sinful nature of man whose life is polluted down to his very blood. This is exactly as the Book tells us that we have all sinned and fall short of the glory of God (see Rom. 3:23). The plan of redemption is beautifully foreshadowed as well as the prophetic pattern of the Blood, water, and Spirit as the answer for fallen man—for his blood to live! How would this be possible? They would have to be born again and washed in the blood of Jesus and enter into covenant with God.

*I have caused thee to multiply as the bud of the field, and thou hast increased and waxen great, and thou art come to excellent ornaments: thy breasts are fashioned, and thine hair is grown, whereas thou wast naked and bare. Now when I passed by thee, and looked upon thee, behold, thy time was the time of love; and I spread my skirt over thee, and covered thy nakedness: yea, I sware unto thee, and entered into a covenant with thee, saith the Lord God, and thou becamest mine* (Ezekiel 16:7-8).

Notice from these verses that God entered covenant with us through His Blood that takes our polluted, sinful

123

life and gives us new life by declaring, "Live!" (see verse 6). This is redemption, and it is a good place for we who are redeemed to say so! Yet once again, the prophetic pattern of the Blood, water, and Spirit is clearly seen in the following verse in Ezekiel 16.

> *Then washed I thee with water; yea, I throughly washed away thy blood from thee, and I anointed thee with oil* (Ezekiel 16:9).

Notice God washed with water, thoroughly washing away the blood and anointing with oil—the Spirit. Again, a prophetic pattern of what happens through His redemptive plan, but also what is available for us as believers in covenant with God. We are cleansed, forgiven, and given the Holy Spirit and power to minister to others.

## THE PASSOVER AND THE BLOOD, WATER, AND SPIRIT

The Passover is an incredible foreshadowing of God's redemptive plan through the shed blood of a lamb—more importantly, His Lamb whom He would send to the earth in the person Jesus Christ, the Lamb of God. Not only do we see the power of God's redemptive plan but once again the prophetic pattern of the Blood, water, and Spirit. The Israelites were to take the blood of their lamb and sprinkle it with hyssop on the doorposts. Hyssop has a watery root that is not brittle, so it was easy to apply the blood without the roots breaking. Once the blood was applied with the watery roots of the hyssop plant on the doorpost, the

Spirit of God would pass over and not allow the destroyer to touch them or their homes.

> *And ye shall take a bunch of hyssop, and dip it in the blood that is in the bason, and strike the lintel and the two side posts with the blood that is in the bason; and none of you shall go out at the door of his house until the morning. For the Lord will pass through to smite the Egyptians; and when he seeth the blood upon the lintel, and on the two side posts, the Lord will pass over the door, and will not suffer the destroyer to come in unto your houses to smite you (Exodus 12:22-23).*

## David's Prayer and the Prophetic Pattern

The last example we are going to look at in the Old Testament is a prayer recorded in Psalm 51 by King David. We once again see this prophetic pattern, but we also see what David knew was available in his life to bring God's forgiveness. After committing adultery with Bathsheba, David begins to cry out for forgiveness starting with the cleansing of blood.

> *Purge me with hyssop, and I shall be clean* (Psalm 51:7a).

Second, he asks for the washing of the water of cleansing by asking God to wash him whiter than snow.

> *Wash me, and I shall be whiter than snow* (Psalm 51:7b).

Third, he asks that God would not withhold His Spirit from him because of his sin.

*Restore unto me the joy of thy salvation; and uphold me with thy free spirit* (Psalm 51:12).

We have seen a few examples from creation and throughout the Old Testament. We will see in the next chapter how this pattern continues throughout the Bible, even with Elijah the prophet and the false prophets of Baal. Yet what about the New Testament? Is this pattern revealed? Yes, absolutely, as we will discover in Jesus' crucifixion and in the book of Acts in the remaining chapters.

## NEW TESTAMENT AND THE PROPHETIC PATTERN

As we examine the prophetic pattern of the Blood, water, and Spirit in the New Testament, one such example is revealed in the book of Hebrews.

*Let us draw near with a true heart in full assurance of faith, having our hearts sprinkled from an evil conscience, and our bodies washed with pure water* (Hebrews 10:22).

Notice the pattern in this verse as it mentions drawing near with a true heart or *spirit*, followed by being sprinkled from an evil conscience through the *Blood* and washed with pure *water*.

This prophetic pattern is also shown at the beginning of Jesus' public ministry and His baptism by John the

Baptist. This prophetic pattern of the Blood, water, and Spirit is clearly seen. It begins as John is baptizing people in the River Jordan and sees Jesus arriving to be baptized and makes a reference to the Blood that the Lord would shed by declaring Jesus as the Lamb of God.

> *The next day John seeth Jesus coming unto him, and saith, Behold the Lamb of God, which taketh away the sin of the world* (John 1:29).

It is followed by the pattern of the water in Jesus' baptism as John baptizes Him.

> *Now when all the people were baptized, it came to pass, that Jesus also being baptized, and praying, the heaven was opened* (Luke 3:21).

Last, the Holy Spirit comes in the form of the dove, which brings a complete picture of the Blood, water, and Spirit at the beginning of Jesus' ministry.

> *And the Holy Ghost descended in a bodily shape like a dove upon him, and a voice came from heaven, which said, Thou art my beloved Son; in thee I am well pleased* (Luke 3:22).

## WATER TO WINE

We looked at the beginning of Jesus' ministry, but how about Jesus' first miracle? We certainly see this pattern is established when He changed the water to wine at the wedding at Cana (see John 2:1-9). Let's look a little more closely at this as it reveals the fullness of life for the believer.

127

It's significant that Jesus' first miracle took place at a marriage supper or wedding feast; it speaks of how we become married or covenanted to Jesus when we are born again through the Blood. When Jesus heard that the guests were out of wine, He instructed that the empty water pots be filled to the brim with water. This represents our condition without the Lord—we are empty water pots that need to be filled with the water of salvation and our new life in Christ. Once we receive Him as our Lord and Savior, we become a new creation in Him!

> *Therefore, if anyone is in Christ, he is a new creation; old things have passed away; behold, all things have become new* (2 Corinthians 5:17 NKJV).

Jesus also spoke of this water in what He told the woman to whom He ministered at the well.

> *But the water that I shall give him shall be in him a well of water springing up into everlasting life* (John 4:14b).

Notice He said, "It shall be in them," meaning there is no other way to fill the emptiness inside us apart from Jesus. People try all manner of things in search of "fullness," but Jesus is the only way we will ever truly be satisfied and filled.

After the pots were filled with water, we're told that it was turned to wine. Wine in this story has two significant meanings in relation to the prophetic pattern we are discussing. First, the wine is also a prophetic type of the Blood as it is often called the blood of grapes. In Genesis 49:11, wine is specifically called *"the blood of grapes."* In the book of Revelation, when the vine of the earth was harvested and the grapes cast into the winepress of God and trampled, it says that *"blood came out of the winepress"* (Rev. 14:20). Finally, wine was likened to blood when Jesus took the cup at the Last Supper, saying this is "the cup of the New Testament in My Blood."

Second, we are to be filled with the "new wine" baptism of the Holy Spirit that's spoken of in Isaiah 65: *"New wine is found in the cluster, and one saith, Destroy it not; for a blessing is in it"* (Isa. 65:8). This new wine is also a reference to Acts 2:13, when those who'd been filled with the Holy Spirit were accused of being drunk. Remember that Peter clarified for them that this was not drunkenness, but rather a "new wine" infilling of the Holy Spirit and the fulfillment of God's promise to pour out His Spirit on all flesh (see Acts 2:17).

Finally, as we look at the result of the water turning to wine, the wine was drawn out of the water pots and served to the guests. This "new wine" was the *best* wine! This has a couple symbolic meanings we need to consider in context of the prophetic pattern we are discovering. First, this example of Jesus' first miracle is an amazing prophetic pattern of the Blood, water, and Spirit revealing God's plan for us. Let's look at the connection to this miracle at a wedding, filling empty water pots, and a supernatural transformation into new wine and our lives today.

Like the empty water pots, our lives are empty without salvation through the blood of Jesus. Once we are saved, that emptiness and searching is the hunger satisfied in us when we accept Jesus. In addition, even though we are saved we need to be filled with the water of His Word as it is our life and refreshing (see Eph. 5:26). Yet it isn't enough to just have our empty lives saved and filled; we need transformation. In other words, we need the supernatural touch and outpouring of the Holy Spirit on our lives like Jesus turning the water into wine. This transformation is not just for us but is to be poured out like Jesus instructed in the power of His Spirit.

When we are born again, it is a covenant through His Blood as serious and committed as a marriage, as we see in the marriage Jesus attended. Then, as empty water pots that He has filled, we need transformation or conversion through the filling of water—that is, baptism in the water of conversion. Finally, we are to be filled with Spirit through pouring out the "new wine" of the Holy Spirit's power. This enables us daily to go forth, empowered and able to serve "the best wine"—demonstrating signs, wonders, and the power of the Holy Spirit as we minister to others!

This is exactly the second example we can see from Jesus' first miracle. It reveals the powerful Holy Spirit outpouring and baptism on the day of Pentecost. Remember, Jesus said this regarding the Holy Spirit that His Father would send in His name:

> *He that believeth on me, as the scripture hath said, out of his belly shall flow rivers of living*

*water. (But this spake he of the Spirit, which they that believe on him should receive: for the Holy Ghost was not yet given; because that Jesus was not yet glorified)* (John 7:38-39).

Remember the "new wine," which is a type of the Holy Spirit, was to be poured out from empty vessels after experiencing a supernatural transformation just like what happened to those in the upper room. They were transformed—no longer empty like the empty water pots, but filled with the Spirit and even seen as drunk with "new wine." Like with Jesus' first miracle, it wasn't enough for them to be filled with the Spirit but they had to be poured out. This is the Holy Spirit baptism available to all believers once they are saved. Yet it is more than just a Holy Spirit outpouring but also God approving of something and witnessing to that approval! We will look at this more in the next chapter.

We have unpacked some of the amazing benefits He's provided through His Blood, but we must not stop there. Fifty days after Jesus offered Himself as the perfect sacrificial Lamb, the Day of Pentecost arrived, and the Holy Spirit was poured out just like the water pots! Would this prophetic pattern once again be revealed on the Day of Pentecost? Yes, Pentecost showed that God's plan of redemption had been fulfilled. In addition, this prophetic pattern was unveiled so that we would walk in the fullness of what has been provided in our covenant with the Lord and add our agreement to His prophetic pattern of the Blood, water, and Spirit!

CHAPTER EIGHT

# PENTECOST AND THE BLOOD, WATER, AND SPIRIT

As we examine what happened at Pentecost, we will again see a clear and powerful revelation of this prophetic pattern, and you may be surprised by what God communicates through this. Before we do, let's talk about fire and how God used it in blood sacrifices offered to Him. The reason we need to consider why God chose fire is because it will help us understand more in-depth what Pentecost meant to God and should mean for us. What happened on the Day of Pentecost is not just a story or experience that those in the upper room encountered. It is how God showed His approval of the Blood shed at Calvary by Jesus Christ. It reveals that God approved; now we must add our agreement, meaning we must add the Holy Spirit's baptism to our Christian life. We will talk about this more in-depth and how it applies to our lives and the prophetic pattern of the Blood, water, and Spirit.

We can see God showing approval of a blood sacrifice by fire all the way from Abraham's day forward. God approved a blood sacrifice by sending His manifest presence, oftentimes by fire. From as far back as the Garden, God determined that animal sacrifices would serve as a way to cover sin. Reading through the Old Testament, it's easy to see that offering sacrifices was part of everyday life for the people of Israel. What can be easy to miss is the way God showed His approval of sacrifices by sending His fire. We see this in the lives of David, Solomon, and others.

Of course, the most dramatic time that God answered by fire was on Mount Carmel when Elijah had a stand-off with the prophets of Baal (see 1 Kings 18). Elijah was so confident in his God that he mocked those 400 false prophets because he was fully assured that the Lord would send His fire and show Himself to be the one true God.

> Then you call on the name of your gods, and I will call on the name of the Lord; and the God who answers by fire, He is God. So all the people answered and said, "It is well spoken" (1 Kings 18:24 NKJV).

After Elijah had prepared the sacrifice (1 Kings 18:30-35), he prayed to the Lord (1 Kings 18:36-37), and then the fire of the Lord fell:

> *Then the fire of the Lord fell, and consumed the burnt sacrifice, and the wood, and the stones, and the dust, and licked up the water that was in the trench* (1 Kings 18:38).

Elijah said to the prophets of Baal that the proof that the Lord was God and that He approved of the blood sacrifice offered would be that He would answer by fire. However, pay attention to not only the proof of God sending fire but once again discover the prophetic pattern of the Blood, water, and Spirit to reveal *why*. It was to show that God approved of Elijah's sacrifice by answering with the fire of His Spirit.

> *And he put the wood in order, and cut the bullock in pieces* [blood], *and laid him on the wood, and said, Fill four barrels with water, and pour it on the burnt sacrifice, and on the wood.... Hear me, O Lord, hear me, that this people may know that thou art the Lord God, and that thou hast turned their heart back again. Then the fire* [Spirit] *of the Lord fell, and consumed the burnt sacrifice, and the wood, and the stones, and the dust, and licked up the water that was in the trench* (1 Kings 18:33, 37-38).

Let's look at how the prophetic pattern is revealed and what it points to in our lives. The blood was evident in the cutting of the bullock pieces and laying them on the wood—prophetically speaking, as Jesus was laid upon the cross for our redemption. These four barrels were to be filled with water three times and poured onto the sacrifice. Sounds like the empty water pots Jesus filled with water in His first miracle and poured out. Again, this is a type of the prophetic pattern, including Pentecost, the Holy Spirit outpouring, and God's approval.

> *And he put the wood in order, and cut the bullock in pieces, and laid him on the wood, and said, Fill four barrels with water, and pour it on the burnt sacrifice, and on the wood. And he said, Do it the second time. And they did it the second time. And he said, Do it the third time. And they did it the third time* (1 Kings 18:33-34).

Notice the prophetic act of filling the four barrels with water and pouring them out three times equals the number twelve. The number twelve signifies the Kingdom of God, as seen in the twelve gates in the heavenly Jerusalem or the twelve apostles of the Lamb. What this prophetic act reveals is that we who are born into the Kingdom of God must pour out our lives testifying of Jesus Christ. That is not the only thing, but when we are born again into the Kingdom through the Blood, like the water pots we discussed in Jesus' first miracle, we need the infilling of the water of His Word.

The water in the barrels that Elijah instructed them to fill was then poured out, and the next thing that happened was something supernatural—God sent His fire. Why fire? It was to show not just God's power but His approval! He was showing that He approved of the blood sacrifice Elijah offered and that the Lord was indeed the one and only true God in the face of the false prophets of Baal. This was proof, or a witness from heaven, that the Lord approved of the blood sacrifice. This approving and foreshadowing was to prophetically reveal the supernatural fire that would come on the day of Pentecost to show God's approval—not of the blood of a bullock, like with Elijah, but rather His approval of the Blood of the Lamb of God, Jesus!

Another example that solidifies our understanding is found in David and Solomon. God once again answered them by fire when they made their offerings to Him.

> *And David built there an altar unto the Lord, and offered burnt offerings and peace offerings, and called upon the Lord; and he answered him from heaven by fire upon the altar of burnt offering* (1 Chronicles 21:26).
>
> *Now when Solomon had made an end of praying, the fire came down from heaven, and consumed the burnt offering and the sacrifices; and the glory of the Lord filled the house* (2 Chronicles 7:1).

In both examples with David and Solomon, how do we know that God approved of the blood sacrifice being offered? It was once again through God witnessing or showing He approved by sending fire from heaven. Sounds like Pentecost, doesn't it? As God witnessed to the sacrifice of blood with fire, He did the same by approving of Jesus' Blood on the Day of Pentecost. He did this by pouring out His Spirit in the manifestation of fire that settled upon the hundred and twenty in the upper room that day. All were filled with Spirit, speaking in tongues!

> *And when the day of Pentecost was fully come, they were all with one accord in one place. And suddenly there came a sound from heaven as of a rushing mighty wind, and it filled all the house where they were sitting. And there appeared unto them cloven tongues like as of fire, and it sat upon each of them. And they were all filled with the Holy Ghost, and began to speak with other tongues, as the Spirit gave them utterance* (Acts 2:1-4).

Let's look at another example of God showing His approval by answering by fire in the story of Cain and Abel. It not only shows us just how important our heart and offerings are to the Lord, it also shows how important Pentecost's outpouring of the Holy Spirit and fire is to Him.

## SACRIFICES OF CAIN AND ABEL

If we look back even further in Scripture, I believe we can assume God answered Abel by fire when Abel offered his blood sacrifice. After Adam, his sons Cain and Abel were the next ones who would offer sacrifices to God. Abel was called a *"keeper of sheep"* and his brother Cain was a *"tiller of the ground"* (Gen. 4:2).

> *The Lord accepted Abel and his gift, but he did
> not accept Cain and his gift. So Cain became very
> angry and felt rejected* (Genesis 4:4b-5 NCV).

Looking more closely at these two offerings, God had
not required an offering of vegetables, but Cain gave the
fruit of the ground (see Gen. 4:3). We're told that Abel
brought fat portions from some of the firstborn of his
flock, which would have been a blood sacrifice in obedi-
ence to what God required (see Gen. 4:4).

Notice that God accepted Abel's sacrifice and rejected
Cain's. How would God have expressed His approval of
Abel's offering? We can assume that He sent fire to con-
sume Abel's sacrifice. Remember, Elijah called God *"the
God who answers by fire"* (1 Kings 18:24 NKJV).

God sent a witness that Abel's offering was approved.
What was that proof? Look at what Hebrews 11:4 tells us:

> *It was faith that made Abel offer to God a better
> sacrifice than Cain's. Through his faith he won
> God's approval as a righteous man, because God
> himself approved of his gifts. By means of his faith
> Abel still speaks, even though he is dead* (GNT).

What would have brought the fire of God? The fire
would have come when Abel offered his best lamb, the firstborn of his flock (see Gen. 4:4). But why didn't God send
fire to consume Cain's vegetable offering? It was because
there was no blood offered from the vegetables. Blood
could only be offered from an animal sacrifice.

*And Adam knew Eve his wife; and she conceived, and bare Cain, and said, I have gotten a man from the Lord. And she again bare his brother Abel. And Abel was a keeper of sheep, but Cain was a tiller of the ground. And in process of time it came to pass, that Cain brought of the fruit of the ground an offering unto the Lord. And Abel, he also brought of the firstlings of his flock and of the fat thereof. And the Lord had respect unto Abel and to his offering* (Genesis 4:1-4).

## THE WAY OF CAIN

Let's look a little more closely at Cain, because the Bible warns us about going "the way of Cain." We must be aware of what I call the "Cain spirit."

*Woe unto them! for they have gone in the way of Cain, and ran greedily after the error of Balaam for reward, and perished in the gainsaying of Core* (Jude 11).

So what is the "way of Cain" today and how does it apply to the pattern of the Blood, water, and Spirit or the Day of Pentecost? The "way of Cain" or the "Cain spirit" refers to doing things on your own terms and treating what God requires as not important to Him or the individual, as we saw with Cain and his offering to God.

In like manner, the "way of Cain" would be to treat the Blood of salvation, the water of baptism, and the baptism of the Holy Spirit with the evidence of speaking in tongues as something that is not necessary or on our terms. We need to be careful that we don't treat any of these elements of our life in God as optional or not important to God or to our lives. It is not optional to avoid the Blood and not live a converted life in Christ. Neither is it optional to be filled with the Holy Spirit and speak in tongues like on the day of Pentecost. This is not to imply you won't make heaven or God will not be happy with you. It is rather to reveal why this prophetic pattern is being revealed in Scripture and why we need to add our agreement by appropriating this into our lives!

Remember the agreement of the Blood, water, and Spirit mentioned in First John 5:8. This means we must add our agreement by going deeper and not thinking of them as optional in our lives. When we do, we are going the way of Cain. Cain mocked or disregarded the importance of the Blood and God's witness of His fire/presence. Some people do this today when it comes to the Blood of Jesus, the baptism of the Holy Spirit, and receiving His gifts.

Scripture also tells us that Cain was influenced by the devil, to the point of murdering his own brother.

> *Not as Cain, who was of that wicked one, and slew his brother. And wherefore slew he him? Because his own works were evil, and his brother's righteous* (1 John 3:12).

In Genesis 4, God spoke to Cain and asked him, "If you do what is right, will you not be accepted?" From the wording of this question, I think God had taught Adam, and Adam had taught his sons. Cain would have known what was right—otherwise, God would not have phrased His question this way.

> *If you do what is right, will you not be accepted? But if you do not do what is right, sin is crouching at your door; it desires to have you, but you must rule over it* (Genesis 4:7 NIV).

Both Cain and Abel would have been taught the right thing of blood sacrifices by their father Adam, as the Lord taught him with the animal skins dripping in blood (see Gen. 3). Let's look at Abel's sacrifice and how it was different from Cain's:

1.  Abel did the right thing and brought the sacrifice.

    *And Abel also brought an offering—fat portions from some of the firstborn of his flock* (Genesis 4:4a NIV).

2.  Only certain parts of the animal were considered acceptable for sacrifice, and Abel brought his animal sacrifice according to what was acceptable to God.

    *The priest shall burn them on the altar as a food offering, a pleasing aroma. All the fat is the Lord's. This is a lasting ordinance for the generations to come, wherever you live: You must not eat any fat or any blood* (Leviticus 3:16-17 NIV).

3. Abel only brought some of his flock. He did not bring all his flock.

   *The rich are not to give more than a half shekel and the poor are not to give less when you make the offering to the Lord to atone for your lives* (Exodus 30:15 NIV).

4. Abel offered a firstborn.

   *All the firstborn males of your livestock belong to the Lord* (Exodus 13:12b NIV).

5. The animal that Abel offered was his. Because it belonged to him, he was making a personal sacrifice.

   *All the firstborn males of your livestock belong to the Lord* (Exodus 13:12b NIV).

6. He offered an animal of the flock. He didn't offer a fish, owl, dog, or pig. How did Abel know to offer a sheep or goat?

   *When anyone among you brings an offering to the Lord, bring as your offering an animal from either the herd or the flock* (Leviticus 1:2b NIV).

In addition to the six things that the Bible tells us in Genesis 4:4, it also says that Abel came by faith. Cain and Abel had both witnessed their father's faith and example of giving blood sacrifice and offerings.

*By faith Abel offered to God a better sacrifice than Cain* (Hebrews 11:4a NASB).

So we see that Cain went his own way and was disobedient to God, refusing to offer the sacrifice He required. But Abel's sacrifice was right in the sight of God and God showed His approval and acceptance of it through sending His fire.

Like each of the instances of God sending fire as His approval of sacrifices offered by David, Solomon, and Elijah, Abel's sacrifice was a foreshadowing of Jesus being offered not only as an acceptable sacrifice, but our perfect sacrifice. God would also send fire to express His approval of Jesus' sacrifice offered at Calvary. He waited until the Day of Pentecost to send His fire!

# CHAPTER NINE

# PENTECOST AND THE APPROVAL OF GOD

The God who answers and approves by sending fire is clearly understood in the examples we have seen throughout Scripture. It is also one of the reasons the prophetic pattern of the Blood, water, and Spirit is shown throughout Scripture. It is to not only show what is available in the life of every believer but why certain things happened to Jesus on the cross. It was not only to fulfill God's redemptive plan, but to establish the Lord's pattern in our lives. Yet even more powerfully, it shows prophetically why God would send fire and pour out His Spirit on Pentecost. This was all to reveal that the God who answers by fire would once again show His approval of a sacrifice—the very Blood sacrifice of His Son. He would do as He had done before so there would be no question as to His thoughts concerning the bloody crucifixion and sacrifice of His Son, Jesus. He would answer from heaven in the fire of His witness shown in the Holy Spirit coming. This was not the only witness or approval of His Blood sacrifice offered to man. In the mouth of two or three witnesses, His sacrifice would be established.

> But if he will not hear thee, then take with thee one or two more, that in the mouth of two or three witnesses every word may be established (Matthew 18:16).

How about in a hundred mouths of tongue-talkers endued with a supernatural fire from heaven?

> And in those days Peter stood up in the midst of the disciples, and said, (the number of names together were about an hundred and twenty) (Acts 1:15).

They would not only add their agreement, but they would each have the fire on their head individually!

> And there appeared unto them cloven tongues like as of fire, and it sat upon each of them. And they were all filled with the Holy Ghost, and began to speak with other tongues, as the Spirit gave them utterance (Acts 2:3-4).

I believe the fire was not only to signify God's approval. By magnifying God supernaturally with their mouths, they were saying, "God, the Blood is worthy. Here is proof—not just in the fire of the Holy Spirit on our heads but His utterance of tongues in our mouths!"

God was answering again by the fire of the Holy Ghost because of a Blood sacrifice offered Him. The precious Blood of Jesus offered at Calvary would be the last and final sacrifice and no longer would require the blood of animals (see Heb. 9:12). We have a powerful Blood covenant approved and agreed upon by God Himself! We add our agreement and approval by entering this covenant when we are saved, but it doesn't stop there. We further add our agreement to this Blood covenant with our Father through Jesus Christ by accepting and receiving the Holy Spirit's baptism with the evidence of speaking in tongues.

All this was made powerfully available at the cross and because of the cross. It is why once again we see this prophetic pattern of the Blood, water, and Spirit with the crucifixion of Jesus. It was to point to how powerful, sacred, and redeeming the Blood of Jesus is. It was so much so that God would show it by answering with fire on the Day of Pentecost and have a hundred and twenty add their agreement by the supernatural language of speaking in tongues and magnifying God.

The pattern of the Blood, water, and Spirit is to show what God has made available to us and, in addition, what we must add our agreement to in our lives. Saved by the Blood, converted and maturing through the water, and living a Spirit-filled life, speaking in tongues, and demonstrating His power through signs and wonders! All of this because Jesus was willing to suffer and be the final sacrifice of Blood ever offered.

## THE HOLY SPIRIT AS WITNESS

This is why at the crucifixion, after they pierced Jesus' side, blood and water flowed out from it.

> *But one of the soldiers pierced His side with a spear, and immediately blood and water came out* (John 19:34 NASB).

Here with Jesus on the cross, we have two of the three elements of our pattern—Blood and water. But what about the Spirit in the pattern at Jesus' crucifixion? We find it when Jesus said, "Father, into thy hands I give My Spirit." However, it is also seen on the Day of Pentecost, when God the Father waited for Jesus to ascend after His resurrection from the grave and then sent the Holy Spirit. The Holy Spirit outpouring was also the Holy Spirit witnessing to the Blood and water when Jesus offered Himself on the cross and they pierced His side with Blood and water flowing. This is clear when we know the Scripture reveals that the Holy Spirit is the one who bears witness to the water *and* the Blood.

One such example is when the Holy Spirit bore witness to the water at the time of Jesus' baptism after the announcement of Jesus being the Lamb of God who, through His Blood, would take away the sins of the world! (See John 1:29.)

*Now when all the people were baptized, it came to pass, that Jesus also being baptized, and praying, the heaven was opened, and the Holy Ghost descended in a bodily shape like a dove upon him, and a voice came from heaven, which said, Thou art my beloved Son; in thee I am well pleased* (Luke 3:21-22).

Then again, on the Day of Pentecost the Holy Spirit also bore witness to the Blood! As we saw, fire was the consistent way that God witnessed or approved of an offering of a blood sacrifice. When the fire of the Holy Ghost fell on Pentecost, God was showing that Jesus' shed Blood, as the final sacrifice, was approved and pleasing.

*And suddenly there came a sound from heaven as of a rushing mighty wind, and it filled all the house where they were sitting. And there appeared unto them cloven tongues like as of fire, and it sat upon each of them. And they were all filled with the Holy Ghost, and began to speak with other tongues, as the Spirit gave them utterance* (Acts 2:2-4).

Do you see this pattern and just how important it is? Notice that at the crucifixion we see the water and the Blood. Yet it was the outpouring of the Holy Spirit at Pentecost when the Spirit ultimately bore witness to both the water and the Blood. Again we see the complete pattern—Blood, water, and Spirit!

Pay close attention to Peter's message after the Holy Spirit was poured out. He explains this prophetic pattern of the Blood, water, and Spirit that we have examined throughout Scripture. It was all pointing to Jesus, the cross, and this powerful day of Pentecost. Following the Holy Spirit outpouring on the Day of Pentecost in Acts 2, Peter explains this in detail in his sermon. He references the Blood sacrifice in verse 36:

> *Therefore let all the house of Israel know assuredly, that God hath made the same Jesus, whom ye have crucified, both Lord and Christ.*

Water baptism is mentioned in verses 37-38a:

> *Now when they heard this, they were pricked in their heart, and said unto Peter and to the rest of the apostles, Men and brethren, what shall we do? Then Peter said unto them, Repent, and be baptized every one of you in the name of Jesus Christ for the remission of sins.*

And finally, in verses 38-39, Peter describes the Holy Spirit:

> *And you will receive the gift of the Holy Spirit. The promise is for you and your children and for all who are far off, everyone whom the Lord our God calls to himself—for all whom the Lord our God will call* (NIV).

He's talking about us here! When Peter explained, "This is that!" (see Acts 2:16), he was declaring that the outpouring of the Holy Spirit and speaking in tongues was the approval of Jesus' sacrifice. This prophetic pattern was not only clearly seen as he preached, but it was letting them know they must add their agreement to not just one but all three. They were to do this by receiving and appropriating them in their lives. This is no different for us as believers today!

Though many have dismissed it, the outpouring of the Holy Spirit at Pentecost is critical to us as believers. In Peter's sermon, he was showing us exactly the prophetic progression and pattern for our lives today! We must be careful not to reject the outpouring of the Holy Spirit and speaking in tongues. Remember, the Holy Spirit baptism was God's approval of His Blood sacrifice through Jesus. This Holy Spirit baptism is to be received by us today as we are to be filled with His Spirit and speak in tongues. This is adding our agreement to His Blood through salvation, and our agreement to His Holy Spirit and speaking in tongues is fulfilling this prophetic pattern. Therefore, when God sent His Holy Spirit, it was so much more than just giving us the ability to speak in tongues. It wasn't just witnessing to the fact that God kept His promise by sending the Holy Spirit, but also that He kept His promise through the Blood! We are not to pick and choose, but must add our full agreement to the Blood, and to the water, and finally to the Spirit and His baptism.

When the Holy Spirit came on the Day of Pentecost, it was (and still is) evidence of God's approval of Jesus as the ultimate and final sacrifice! God clearly voiced His approval of Jesus as our perfect, spotless Lamb. When churches, pastors, or believers resist, mock, or deny the baptism of the Holy Spirit, they are insulting the Blood sacrifice of Jesus. It's so important that we are in agreement with God about this. We should never exclude, quench, ban, or deny the Blood of Jesus or the Holy Spirit and His baptism. When we teach against the baptism of the Holy Spirit, we are insulting the holiest sacrifice, Jesus Himself—the sacrifice that God has absolutely accepted for all eternity.

The coming of the Holy Spirit at Pentecost and the infilling of the Holy Spirit is a sacred and holy thing. Those who were present that day were shaken to the core when the mighty rushing wind blew through the upper room! Throughout the Old Testament, we see people having the same kind of reactions when God's presence came and He accepted men's sacrifices. Here are a couple examples:

> *For it came about when the flame went up from the altar toward heaven, that the angel of the Lord ascended in the flame of the altar. When Manoah and his wife saw this, they fell on their faces to the ground* (Judges 13:20 NASB).
>
> *Then the fire of the Lord fell and consumed the burnt offering and the wood and the stones and the dust, and licked up the water that was in the trench. When all the people saw it, they fell on their faces; and they said, "The Lord, He is God; the Lord, He is God"* (1 Kings 18:38-39 NASB).

We can get more understanding of how the Holy Spirit and His baptism are the witness of God's approval of Jesus when we look again more closely at Peter's sermon on the Day of Pentecost.

When the Holy Spirit was poured out that day and those present began speaking in other tongues, the onlookers accused Jesus' followers of being drunk, but Peter stood up and explained:

> *For these are not drunken, as ye suppose, seeing it is but the third hour of the day. But this is that which was spoken by the prophet Joel; and it shall come to pass in the last days, saith God, I will pour out of my Spirit upon all flesh: and your sons and your daughters shall prophesy, and your young men shall see visions, and your old men shall dream dreams* (Acts 2:15-17).

Peter's words, *"this is that,"* reminded the people of what the prophet Joel had spoken—that God had promised He would pour out His Spirit upon man in the last days. "This is that" was the baptism of the Holy Spirit; it was God answering the offering of Jesus' sacrifice by sending His Holy Spirit fire! As Peter continued on, he presented the truths of Scripture concerning Jesus' life, death, and resurrection.

I am not meaning to be redundant when I point out the verses from His sermon again, but I want to really drive home how important this prophetic pattern is and should be in our lives. We need the Blood, water, and His Spirit.

This means we receive His Spirit by speaking in tongues—adding our agreement and approval to the sacrifice of Blood Jesus offered!

In verse 39, Peter tells them that the promise is for them, their children, and *"to all that are afar off"*—this means us. Peter was declaring that this promise of the Holy Spirit was not just for those who were present that day, but it would be available for everyone the Lord would ever call to Himself throughout all of history! God's intention has always been that we would receive salvation, but also the baptism of the Holy Spirit, and therefore be able to live lives full of His power and presence.

We would be foolish to ignore it or dismiss it as a one-time event that only occurred in the book of Acts. Let's keep testifying and witnessing to His Blood, but also His Spirit, every time we open our mouths and speak in tongues. No wonder the devil tries to discredit it, stop it, and even tries to take credit for speaking in tongues as if it is of the devil himself. He hates hearing us speak in tongues as it reminds him of the Blood of Jesus that whipped him and stripped him of his power. He is the biggest loser today as he lost everything God gave him and became a defeated foe. He knows what the Blood accomplished and the benefits of the covenant to us believers. He doesn't want to be reminded of it, so he talks people out of speaking in tongues. You know why? He doesn't want you to add your agreement! If you do and become filled with the Spirit and speak in tongues, you are adding your agreement to the Blood. In addition, every time you open your mouth to speak in tongues you are witnessing to the powerful Blood covenant of Jesus Christ!

## WHAT HAPPENED ON PENTECOST?

No one who was present in the upper room that day had any idea of what they were about to experience when the Holy Spirit would be poured out on them. They'd never experienced anything like this. When He came, He came as a mighty, rushing wind that filled the whole place. Immediately following this, tongues of fire showed up and rested on each of them. Imagine what that must have felt like! What were they to make of this? But we know that they recognized the presence of the Lord because Peter had great clarity and explained this outpouring in great detail, declaring it was the promise of God fulfilled.

Of course, there were others there who did not recognize the Lord in this event as they accused Jesus' followers of acting drunk. But for those who'd been obedient and waited and prayed as Jesus had instructed, He poured out His Spirit in a powerful way. Acts tells us that *all* who were there in the upper room were filled and spoke in tongues, even Mary, Jesus' mother (see Acts 1:14). God also gave a supernatural sign when some people heard others speaking in tongues, but it was their own native language! Through all of these things, it was obvious that God was at work among those who continued to follow Him.

When the tongues of fire came and rested on those who were present, it was the Holy Spirit who gave the words, but the people who spoke them out. These tongues of fire came as a result of Jesus' Blood being shed on the cross when He was crucified. Remember what Peter told the onlookers in Acts 2:36: *"the same Jesus, whom ye have crucified."*

The Holy Spirit came as a witness, as God's approval of Jesus as the final sacrifice! And because the promise of the Holy Spirit is also for us, when we speak in tongues we are testifying all over again of Jesus' shed Blood and God's approval of it! Jesus told His disciples that they would be His witnesses—witnesses of His Blood, but also of His power! We witness by demonstrations of His power and by speaking in tongues. This is why we *speak* in tongues—it is an act of testifying and agreeing with the Lord! To tie this back in to the Blood, water, and Spirit pattern, a believer who is saved by the Blood, baptized in water, and filled with the Holy Spirit (speaking in tongues) is following the biblical pattern that agrees in the earth.

> *But ye shall receive power, after that the Holy Ghost is come upon you: and ye shall be witnesses unto me both in Jerusalem, and in all Judaea, and in Samaria, and unto the uttermost part of the earth* (Acts 1:8).

Because of the tremendous power we receive when we are baptized in the Holy Spirit, the enemy does everything he can to keep us from it. The devil hates everything about Pentecost, and he hates it when we who are baptized in the Holy Ghost and speak in tongues. Why? Because it reminds him of the Blood that overcame him! If he had known what was about to take place, he never would have crucified the Lord.

*And they overcame him by the blood of the Lamb,*
*and by the word of their testimony; and they*
*loved not their lives unto the death* (Revelation
12:11).

We see this all the way back in the book of Exodus at
the first Passover, as the blood on the doorposts defeated
the symbol of the Egyptians (the serpent), and the death
angel passed over God's people, not allowing them to be
harmed. Jesus is still the one who crushes the serpent's head
(see Gen. 3:15), and His Blood will always defeat the devil!

God offered the holy Blood of Jesus, His Son, as a free
gift to all mankind, and He chose the most holy thing to
be a witness of His approval—His Holy Spirit! This is why
it grieves God when people discount Pentecost or speak
against the baptism of the Holy Spirit and speaking in
tongues. Every time we pray in tongues, we are adding our
agreement to what God endorses and approves of. This is
more powerful than we realize!

## PENTECOST'S FIRE AND THE BLOOD OF JESUS

When God would approve of a blood sacrifice in Scripture,
as we mentioned, He would show that by answering with
fire from heaven. This is exactly what you saw on Pentecost
as the Holy Spirit was poured out and tongues of fire settled upon those in the upper room that day.

Why did that happen? It was to show that the Blood
of Jesus was truly enough, and He alone was worthy with
His Blood to pay for our sins through the cross. Heaven

testified of it by sending fire from above to witness that God approved of the sacrifice of His Son's Blood. This is why they spoke in tongues. It is because "out of the mouth of two and three witness let every word be established." When they spoke in that heavenly language that day in the upper room, and when we speak in tongues today, it is witnessing to the fact that the Blood of Jesus is holy, worthy, and more than enough to pay for man's sins and give us eternal life. That is why when someone attacks speaking in tongues, rejects it, and says it is not for today or, worse yet, that it is of the devil, they grieve the heart of God. They are essentially saying the Blood of Jesus wasn't enough and the sign given that it was approved of God—the Spirit and fire of Pentecost—wasn't proof that God was approving and testifying of the Blood sacrifice of the Lamb of God. That's why we should seek to not only be saved by the Blood but converted in our lifestyle, shown not just in our baptism in water but a daily walk with God in righteousness and holiness followed by a powerful life in the spirit and power of the Holy Spirit.

We do this by witnessing to this precious Blood by opening our mouths and praying in tongues. No wonder the devil hates it when we are filled with the Holy Spirit. Even more tormenting to him is when we witness to it by speaking in tongues. It is why he creates false teachings that deny Pentecostal power and the important and initial evidence of the Holy Spirit's outpouring, which is speaking in tongues. He hates that the believer is speaking in this heavenly language that witnesses to the power of our Blood covenant. It torments the devil!

So let's get filled with the Holy Spirit and speak in tongues all the time! If you already have, keep speaking and testifying and witnessing to the Blood. When you do, you are witnessing and adding your agreement in the earth to the Blood, water, and the Spirit.

What would it look like in your life to have a greater honor, respect, and place for the Holy Spirit, for what happened on the Day of Pentecost, and for speaking in tongues? These things are holy and precious to God, so we want to count them as holy and precious too.

# CHAPTER TEN

# THE HOLY SPIRIT BAPTISM AND ADDING OUR AGREEMENT

How exciting to see the importance of Pentecost as God's approval of the Blood of Jesus, and the importance of adding our agreement to it by being filled with the Spirit and speaking in tongues. Remember, it was not just God's approval, but as they magnified God the disciples were testifying as witnesses to Jesus' shed Blood and the Holy Spirit who had come. In the same way, we can add our agreement that we too approve, agree, and accept Jesus' Blood as the final sacrifice and ask Him into our hearts to forgive us of our sins with that precious Blood. It is because we add our agreement that His Blood is worthy to save, heal, deliver, and forgive. Among many benefits of our covenant, we receive the baptism of His Holy Spirit with the evidence of speaking in other tongues.

This wonderful baptism of the Holy Spirit is available to us today, and God desires for us to receive it! Remember what Peter said in Acts 2:39—it is for "all that are afar off" and everyone the Lord calls.

In the modern-day church, there are often two approaches to the baptism of the Holy Spirit. There are those who resist, mock, and quench the Spirit, much like those in Acts 2:13: *"Others mocking said, These men are full of new wine."* And there are those who are open to the Holy Spirit and want to understand more about the baptism. These are like the people spoken of in Acts 2:11-12:

> *"Cretans and Arabs—we hear them speaking in our own languages the mighty works of God." They were all amazed and perplexed, saying to each other, "What does this mean?"* (MEV).

Let's determine that we will be those who seek to know more of the Holy Spirit and to be empowered by Him.

The infilling of the Holy Spirit is so important to our Christian walk. It gives us power to live our lives as Kingdom people and to do powerful exploits that will set others free. Jesus said the Gospel of the Kingdom must be preached to all nations, and that it would be accompanied by signs and wonders. When we are filled with the Holy Spirit, we access this same power that raised Jesus from the dead, and we can literally change the world! Remember that Jesus also told His disciples that:

> *These signs will accompany those who believe: in my name they will cast out demons; they will speak in new tongues; they will pick up serpents with their hands; and if they drink any deadly poison, it will not hurt them; they will lay their hands on the sick, and they will recover* (Mark 16:17-18 ESV).

This is the power available to us through the baptism of the Holy Spirit, and some of the things He said we would do! If these things are not *normal* in your life, I want to encourage you to *think bigger* and go after the fullness of the baptism of the Holy Spirit!

## The River of Power in You

> *"Whoever believes in me, as the Scripture has said, 'Out of his heart will flow rivers of living water.'" Now this he said about the Spirit, whom those who believed in him were to receive, for as yet the Spirit had not been given, because Jesus was not yet glorified* (John 7:38-39 ESV).

Jesus spoke very clearly about the Holy Spirit being a river of power that would live inside of us. He also demonstrated this for us in His own baptism, as the Spirit descended upon Him like a dove. God the Father used this event to show us His heart in giving us His Holy Spirit!

In Matthew 3, Jesus approached John to be baptized by him in the Jordan River. Scripture tells us that when He rose up from the water:

*The heavens were opened to him, and he saw the Spirit of God descending like a dove and coming to rest on him; and behold, a voice from heaven said, "This is my beloved Son, with whom I am well pleased"* (Matthew 3:16b-17 ESV).

At the moment we are baptized in the Holy Spirit, we have the same power living inside of us that Jesus did. In Luke 4:18-19, as Jesus was beginning His ministry on earth, He described seven expressions of the Holy Spirit's power. It's important to know that these seven expressions of power are available to us in the same way they were available to Jesus! Let's take a closer look:

| SEVEN EXPRESSIONS OF THE HOLY SPIRIT'S POWER | WHAT THEY MEAN FOR US |
|---|---|
| 1. *The Spirit of the Lord is upon me, because he hath anointed me* | We have been anointed by God and His Spirit rests upon us. |
| 2. *to preach the gospel to the poor;* | This anointing enables us to share the Gospel and see people come to Christ. |
| 3. *he hath sent me to heal the brokenhearted,* | We bring emotional healing to those with broken hearts. |

| SEVEN EXPRESSIONS OF THE HOLY SPIRIT'S POWER | WHAT THEY MEAN FOR US |
|---|---|
| 4. *to preach deliverance to the captives,* | The power of the Holy Spirit in us means that we can command demons to leave and set people free. |
| 5. *and recovering of sight to the blind,* | We are empowered to minister physical healing and bring spiritual revelation to others. |
| 6. *to set at liberty them that are bruised,* | The anointing power of the Holy Spirit allows us to minister to those who have been bound by trauma and abuse. |
| 7. *to preach the acceptable year of the Lord (Luke 4:18-19).* | We can go forth in the power of the Spirit and proclaim the favor of God and restoration over people's lives. |

These seven expressions of the Holy Spirit's power are also the seven horns of the Lamb that are mentioned in Revelation 5:6b:

*And, lo, in the midst of the throne and of the four beasts, and in the midst of the elders, stood a Lamb as it had been slain, having seven horns and seven eyes, which are the seven Spirits of God sent forth into all the earth.*

This is the incredible, transforming power that lives inside of you as a Spirit-filled believer! Today the seven spirits of God are sent forth into all the earth through *you!* And if God put this earth-shaking power inside of you, He wants you to let it out!

## WHY IS PRAYING IN TONGUES IMPORTANT?

There is a lot of controversy over praying in tongues. Some call it gibberish, while others tap into the depths of the benefits of this kind of prayer. I've found that people tend to fall somewhere along these lines:

- Those who are filled with the Spirit and actively pray in tongues.
- Those who are filled with the Spirit but barely pray in tongues.
- Those who are filled with the Spirit but don't pray in tongues.
- Those who are not filled with the Spirit.
- Those who have heard wrong teaching about the infilling of the Spirit and praying in tongues.

We're going to look at why praying in tongues is so important, and then we will examine some of the most common points of wrong teaching about it.

First, we need to pray in tongues because we need the Holy Spirit's power. Whenever we pray this way, we stir up (activate) the Spirit inside us. In John 7:38-39, Jesus spoke about the power of the Holy Ghost that would be in you and flow out of you:

*"He that believeth on me, as the scripture hath said, out of his belly shall flow rivers of living water." (But this spake he of the Spirit, which they that believe on him should receive: for the Holy Ghost was not yet given; because that Jesus was not yet glorified).*

The way you release that power is when you "break open the fountain of your deep." This is speaking of your spirit in prayer—you break it open by praying in the Spirit. To better understand how this spiritual principle works, let's look at a natural principle and event that took place in Noah's day.

*In the six hundredth year of Noah's life, in the second month, the seventeenth day of the month, the same day were all the fountains of the great deep broken up, and the windows of heaven were opened (Genesis 7:11).*

*And the waters prevailed, and were increased greatly upon the earth; and the ark went upon the face of the waters. And the waters prevailed exceedingly upon the earth; and all the high hills, that were under the whole heaven, were covered. Fifteen cubits upward did the waters prevail; and the mountains were covered. …And the waters prevailed upon the earth an hundred and fifty days (Genesis 7:18-20, 24).*

It was when the fountains of the deep were broken open that the breakthrough came—the heavens opened and the waters prevailed on the earth. This is also what happens when you begin to pray strongly from deep within your spirit. The heavens open over you and your life situations, and you experience victory. God prevails in your situations like the waters did in Noah's day. This is why the Bible says the deep (God) calls unto the deep in us. It is calling out to the breaker spirit within you to reach back to God and be released to flood the earth with His power and glory.

> *Deep calls to deep at the sound of Your waterfalls;*
> *all Your breakers and Your waves have rolled over*
> *me* (Psalm 42:7 NASB).

Genesis 7:18-20 tells us that the heavens opened, but it also says that the waters prevailed. Whatever comes out of heaven prevails over things on the earth! Look at these verses closely to see what happened naturally in the days of Noah, and apply this to yourself regarding how to prevail spiritually:

Verse 18: *And the waters prevailed, and were increased greatly upon the earth.* The waters prevailed and the result was great increase!

Verse 19: *And the waters prevailed exceedingly upon the earth; and all the high hills, that were under the whole heaven, were covered.* The waters prevailed, and the results were exceeding blessings, and the high places, speaking of the demonic high places, were covered!

Verse 20: *Fifteen cubits upward did the waters prevail; and the mountains were covered.* The waters prevailed, and the result was that the mountains were covered, which speaks of the mountains or barriers in your life that seem immovable or too large to overcome!

It is important to pray in tongues often so you can experience God prevailing for you and through you. The apostle Paul said he prayed in tongues more than others because he discovered the benefits and power available to win great spiritual victories. Praying in the Spirit helps to make you spiritually stronger. It manifests a barrier-breaker from within you, and you learn to break through in spiritual realms of conflict. The power to break through any barrier you may be facing is available to you through the Holy Spirit. Breaking open the fountain of your deep is also how you can tap into the Holy Spirit's power. This power is inside of Christians, so we raise up a standard against the devil and win in the battles of life!

## SOME FALSE TEACHING ABOUT THE HOLY SPIRIT'S BAPTISM

You don't have to look far these days to find people who mock the Holy Spirit and erroneously teach about His baptism. Sadly, there are still many who reject this wonderful gift, believing that it is "not for today" or that it is insignificant. Scripture shows us how significant it is to God, and how it is the power behind the ministry of the believer—starting with Jesus, then for His apostles, and all the way down through history to us! Let's see how some of the unsound teaching is clearly refuted by the Word of God.

Listed below are some false beliefs about the Holy Spirit's baptism, and the truths about each of these are included as well:

*False belief: It passed away.*

Truth: First Corinthians 13:8 tells us that knowledge hasn't passed away, and neither has the gift of tongues! And remember Acts 2:38-41, where Peter made it clear that the baptism of the Holy Spirit was for "those that are afar off"—meaning the generations that would follow. Aren't you glad that the power of the Holy Spirit is still available to us today?

*False belief: You have to wait, or tarry, to receive it.*

Truth: Those who teach this are using Luke 24:49 as a reference. But when we look more carefully at that verse, Jesus was instructing His disciples to go to Jerusalem. If this verse justifies waiting for the Holy Spirit, then it would also stand to reason that anyone who wants the baptism of the Holy Spirit should be waiting in Jerusalem! Also, look at Acts 10:44—it says that the Holy Spirit fell *while Peter was speaking.* There was clearly no waiting here! We don't have to wait, but once we know it is available to us, we must go after it!

*False belief: Some receive the baptism of the Holy Spirit, but others don't.*

Truth: On the day of Pentecost, when the mighty rushing wind roared through the upper room, Acts 2:4 tells us that *"they were* all *filled with the Holy Spirit and began to speak in other tongues as the Spirit gave them utterance.*" This false belief is simply confusing the infilling of the Holy Spirit as being the same thing as the gift of tongues that is mentioned in First Corinthians 14, which they are not.

### False belief: When you are saved you have all the Holy Spirit you need.

Truth: If that were the case, there was no reason for Acts 2 to occur. But we see that they were empowered with a power they'd never had before, although they'd been following Jesus for more than three years. In Acts 3, the very next chapter, Peter and John healed the lame beggar—by the power of the Holy Spirit! And in Acts 4, as more were coming to believe in Jesus, we're told that the Holy Spirit came and filled them and gave them boldness:

> *"And now, Lord, look upon their threats and grant to your servants to continue to speak your word with all boldness, while you stretch out your hand to heal, and signs and wonders are performed through the name of your holy servant Jesus." And when they had prayed, the place in which they were gathered together was shaken, and they were all filled with the Holy Spirit and continued to speak the word of God with boldness* (Acts 4:29-31 ESV).

Paul also prays for the Ephesians to receive "the Spirit of wisdom and revelation" (see Eph. 1:17). If they already had "all the Holy Spirit" they needed, Paul would not have prayed this for them! Also, remember the rivers of living water that Jesus spoke of in John 7:38-39—they were not stagnant, they were moving and alive and not always at the same level.

We see these different levels in Ezekiel 47, where the prophet Ezekiel describes the river as having four different levels—ankle deep, knee deep, waist deep, and over his head—deep enough to swim in! This is *increase*, meaning that there is more of the Spirit for us to receive and walk in. Thank God that He always wants the river of the Holy Spirit to be full and overflowing through us!

### False belief: It's of the devil.

Truth: We know this isn't true because it isn't what Jesus said! In Luke 24:49, Jesus said, *"Behold, I send the Promise of My Father upon you; but tarry in the city of Jerusalem until you are endued with power from on high"* (NKJV). This promise is the same as in Luke 11 where Jesus said, *"If ye then, being evil, know how to give good gifts unto your children: how much more shall your heavenly Father give the Holy Spirit to them that ask him?"* (Luke 11:13 KJV).

As we've discussed, Peter explained that the outpouring of the Spirit and speaking in tongues was a fulfillment of what the prophet Joel had spoken (see Acts 2:16, 37-41). This tells us it was from God and not from the devil, because God was doing exactly what He'd promised!

In Acts 8, Simon the sorcerer tried to buy the ability to impart the gift of the Holy Spirit, but think about this for a moment: Simon was a sorcerer. If it was of the devil, he would have already been able to do this!

Also, it is specifically said in Acts 2 that those who spoke in tongues on the Day of Pentecost were magnifying God, not the devil: "*both Jews and proselytes, Cretans and Arabians—we hear them telling in our own tongues the mighty works of God*" (Acts 2:11 ESV). We also see this in Acts 10: "*they were hearing them speaking in tongues and extolling God*" (Acts 10:46 ESV).

### False belief: You can't pray in tongues without an interpretation.

Truth: Scripture makes a distinction between two types of tongues—the public prayer, which is a message from God to an individual or the church body and needs an interpretation for the public assembly, versus private prayer, which doesn't require an interpretation.

This idea that tongues always require an interpretation is simply not true; Paul gave instruction in First Corinthians 14 in reference to the public and local assembly or church meeting. He was teaching them how to use the gift of tongues in an orderly way in a public meeting. It did not refer to the private use of speaking in tongues:

> *Wherefore let him that speaketh in an unknown tongue pray that he may interpret. For if I pray in an unknown tongue, my spirit prayeth, but my understanding is unfruitful* (1 Corinthians 14:13-14).

A few verses later in that same chapter, we again see a reference to praying publicly in tongues:

> *If anyone speaks in a tongue, let there be two or at the most three, each in turn, and let one interpret. But if there is no interpreter, let him keep silent in church, and let him speak to himself and to God* (1 Corinthians 14:27-28 NKJV).

In contrast, the book of Jude speaks of privately praying in tongues:

> *But ye, beloved, building up yourselves on your most holy faith, praying in the Holy Ghost, keep yourselves in the love of God, looking for the mercy of our Lord Jesus Christ unto eternal life* (Jude 1:20-21).

These verses tell us, in addition to many other benefits, that praying in tongues builds us up in our faith, helps to keep us in the love of God, and enables us to recognize and receive God's mercy. Why wouldn't we want this? Who doesn't want to be built up in their faith? Who doesn't want to know the keeping power of the love of God? And which of us doesn't want to know and receive God's mercy? In the hour in which we're living, we can't afford to be without any of these things!

If you've sat under erroneous teaching about the baptism of the Holy Spirit, some of what you've read may sound strange and even make you uncomfortable. But I believe you're not reading this book by accident. I believe the Lord is drawing you and now is your time to respond.

When you do, you are witnessing to the fact that the Blood of Jesus was and is enough. Just as God offered His approval of the Blood by sending the Holy Spirit, in the same way when you receive the Holy Spirit's baptism, you are adding your agreement to God and witnessing to the fact the Blood of Jesus is enough! By speaking in tongues, you fulfill the prophetic pattern that began with you being born again by the Blood, followed by baptism in water and living a holy and changed life, then agreeing to receive this precious gift of the Holy Spirit and speak in tongues. It is not just a heavenly language given; it is also a verbal witness to the Blood sacrifice of Jesus and magnifying God for sending Him. In addition, it is reminding the devil of this worthy Blood sacrifice of the Lamb of God. By speaking in tongues you are witnessing, testifying, and adding your agreement to God's plan of redemption fulfilled in the prophetic pattern of the Blood, water, and Spirit!

No matter where we are in our walk with the Lord, He always has more for us! There are several ways you can respond to God today. If you've never received salvation, today is your day to ask Jesus into your heart to forgive you of your sins and be the Lord of your life. And if you've been saved but haven't been water baptized, this is your time to find a place for that. Maybe everything you've read about the baptism of the Holy Spirit has stirred something inside you. If so, ask the Lord to baptize you in His Spirit and fill you with His power.

Regardless of where you are today, continue to go after the Lord! Press in to be closer than you ever have before, adding your agreement to His approval of Jesus' sacrifice by not only being filled with the Spirit but witnessing to His worthy Blood by speaking in tongues! Don't be afraid of the unfamiliar or of other people's opinions. Be determined to walk in the fullness of life that Jesus died to give you—Blood, water, and Spirit!

I have included the means to add your agreement by giving a brief instruction on how to receive His precious baptism and also how to minister to others:

## Receiving and Ministering the Baptism of the Holy Spirit

Here are several simple steps you can use to receive, or help someone else to receive, the baptism of the Holy Spirit. These steps are patterned after the way people received in the book of Acts.

### 1. Make sure they are a Christian and they have made Jesus their Lord and Savior.

We must be saved before we can receive the baptism of the Holy Spirit. For many, it is helpful to ask them if they are sure they are saved. Some struggle to receive simply because they are not sure they are even right with God.

### 2. Encourage them that this is a biblical promise God wants them to have.

In Acts 2:38-39, Peter encouraged the hearers on the Day of Pentecost that this promise was for them and their children, and it is still for us today (see James 1:17; Heb. 13:8).

### 3. Let them know they are receiving the Holy Spirit, not just tongues.

Speaking in tongues is only the evidence of the Holy Spirit filling them. However, the focus is the Holy Spirit and His power filling their life, not speaking in tongues only.

### 4. Lead them in a prayer.

Truthfully, in most scriptural examples, people didn't pray an actual prayer to receive, but they did need to exercise their faith and be expectant to receive. Often repeating a prayer helps people use their faith for receiving. Remember, God always answers the heart that seeks Him, and He delights in answering our prayers!

### 5. Pray for them and lay hands on them.

If you are alone, you can still receive the baptism of the Holy Spirit! You can simply lay hands on yourself and tell the Lord you want to receive. If you're with someone else, you may want to lay your hands on them and pray for them to receive and gently say, "Receive the Holy Spirit." In the Bible, we find the disciples laying hands on the recipients. However, in some cases they did not. The Holy Spirit just fell on them.

### 6. Tell them to expect to speak in tongues.

Some people are more confident and will instantly start speaking out in tongues. Others need encouraging.

Remember that although the Holy Spirit forms the language, *they* have to do the talking. It often helps to have them open their mouth and move their tongue and stop any speaking in their natural language. Sometimes people will hear unusual syllables or sounds in their heart or mind. Tell them to speak them out without worrying how they sound. It helps if you also start speaking in tongues along with them.

If you are alone and praying to receive for yourself, you should also expect to speak in tongues. Use the above steps as a guideline—open your mouth, move your tongue, and stop speaking in your natural language. As you yield yourself to the Lord, speak out any unusual sounds or syllables without worrying what you sound like.

## Overcoming Any Fears about the Baptism of the Holy Spirit

Here are a few common questions some people may have about the baptism of the Holy Spirit and corresponding answers that can be helpful to share:

### 1. Can I accidentally receive a "wrong" or "evil spirit" instead of the Holy Spirit?

You don't have to worry about getting a "wrong" spirit or a demon instead of the Holy Spirit. Luke 11 says:

> *If a son shall ask bread of any of you that is a father, will he give him a stone? or if he ask a fish, will he for a fish give him a serpent? Or if he shall ask an egg, will he offer him a scorpion? If ye*

*then, being evil, know how to give good gifts unto your children; how much more shall your heavenly Father give the Holy Spirit to them that ask him?* (Luke 11:11-13).

## 2. What if I don't speak in tongues?

If you don't seem to "hear" any syllables in your heart, be bold enough to just move your mouth and make sounds. Isaiah 28:11 says, *"For with stammering lips and another tongue will he speak to this people."* The experience is different for everyone, so if your lips just seem to babble or stammer at first, this is okay. Remember every person's experience may not be the same!

## 3. Are the tongues fake or just in my mind?

Remember that when you speak in tongues, it is *you* who does the speaking, while the Holy Spirit gives the utterance. Acts 19:6 says, *"and* they *spake with tongues."* Who spoke? They did! Yes, it will sound like you, and you will hear the words in your mind too, while the Holy Spirit is forming those sounds into a powerful and supernatural language!

## STRONG SPIRIT, STRONG LIFE

Most of us are very familiar with our natural minds being in control, so allowing your spirit to be in control as you pray in tongues will take some practice. Don't get discouraged— the more you do it, the more you are building up your spirit and before you know it, it will be second nature to you.

As we strengthen our spirits, we allow them to rule over our souls (mind, will, and emotions). You may find your spirit gaining victories over the battles you used to fight in your mind, your will, and your emotions. Now, you might not feel anything or notice this immediately, but over time you will be strengthened, joyful, and full of faith. When our spirits are strong, our faith is built up and we are confident that God will work miracles both within us and for others as we minister to them. Like the disciples, we will go forth empowered as the Lord's witnesses, taking the Gospel to the ends of the earth with signs, wonders, and miracles!

# ABOUT HANK KUNNEMAN

Hank Kunneman pastors Lord of Hosts Church in Omaha, Nebraska, with his wife, Brenda. Together they host a weekly program, *New Level with Hank and Brenda,* on Daystar Television Network. As an author and uncompromising voice for God's Word, he is known for a strong prophetic anointing, preaching, and ministering in meetings and on national television programs. His ministry has truly been marked for accuracy in national and worldwide events.

.